REBEL BUDDHA

reb·el [ré-bəl]
one who questions, resists, refuses to obey, or rises
against the unjust or unreasonable control
of an authority or tradition.

bud·dha [bü´-də]
the awakened mind.

rebel buddha

A GUIDE TO A REVOLUTION OF MIND

Dzogchen Ponlop

SHAMBHALA
BOULDER
2011

Shambhala Publications, Inc.
4720 Walnut Street
Boulder, Colorado 80301
www.shambhala.com

13 12 11 10 9 8 7 6

Printed in the United States of America

♾ This edition is printed on acid-free paper that meets the American National Standards Institute z39.48 Standard.
♻ This book is printed on 30% postconsumer recycled paper.
For more information please visit www.shambhala.com.
Distributed in the United States by Penguin Random House LLC and in Canada by Random House of Canada Ltd

Designed by Gopa & Ted2, Inc.

Library of Congress Cataloging-in-Publication Data
Dzogchen Ponlop, Rinpoche, 1965–
Rebel Buddha: a guide to a revolution of mind / Dzogchen Ponlop.—1st ed.
p.   cm.
Paperback reissue of Rebel Buddha: on the road to freedom.
Includes bibliographical references and index.
ISBN 978-1-59030-929-2 (pbk.: alk. paper)
1. Buddhism—Doctrines. 2. Truth—Religious aspects—Buddhism. I. Title.
BQ4570.F7D96 2011
294.3'4—dc22
2011014791

This book is dedicated to my little rebel buddha,

Raymond Sidarta Wu,

the first generation of my family to be born in America.

contents

REBEL BUDDHA

introduction

REBEL BUDDHA is an exploration of what it means to be free and how we can become free. Although we may vote for the head of our government, marry for love, and worship the divine or mundane powers of our choice, most of us don't really feel free in our day-to-day life. When we talk about freedom, we're also talking about its opposite—bondage, lack of independence, being subject to the control of something or someone outside ourselves. No one likes it, and when we find ourselves in that situation, we quickly start trying to figure out a way around it. Any restriction on our "life, liberty, and pursuit of happiness" arouses fierce resistance. When our happiness and freedom are at stake, we become capable of transforming ourselves into rebels.

There's something of a rebellious streak in all of us. Usually it's dormant, but sometimes it's provoked into expression. If nurtured and guided with wisdom and compassion, it can be a positive force that frees us from fear and ignorance. However, if it manifests neurotically, full of resentment, anger, and self-interest, then it can turn into a destructive force that harms us as much as it does others. When we're confronted with a threat to our freedom or independence and that rebellious streak surfaces, we can choose how to react and channel that energy. It can become part of a contemplative process that leads to insight. Sometimes that insight comes quickly, but it can also take years.

According to the Buddha, our freedom is never in question. We're born free. The true nature of the mind is enlightened wisdom and compassion. Our mind is always brilliantly awake and aware. Nevertheless, we're often plagued by painful thoughts and the emotional unrest that goes with them. We live in states of confusion and fear from which we see no escape. Our problem is that we don't see who we truly are at the deepest level. We don't recognize the power of our enlightened nature. We trust the reality we see before our eyes and accept its validity until something comes along—an illness, accident, or disappointment—to disillusion us. Then we might be ready to question our beliefs and start searching for a more meaningful and lasting truth. Once we take that step, we're starting off on the road to freedom.

On this road, what we free ourselves from is illusion, and what frees us from illusion is the discovery of truth. To make that discovery, we need to enlist the powerful intelligence of our own awake mind and turn it toward our goal of exposing, opposing, and overcoming deception. That is the essence and mission of "rebel buddha": to free us from the illusions we create by ourselves, about ourselves, and from those that masquerade as reality in our cultural and religious institutions.

We start by looking at the dramas in our life, not with our ordinary eyes, but with the eyes of dharma. What is drama, and what is dharma? I guess you could say *drama* is illusion that acts like truth, and *dharma* is truth itself—the way things are, the basic state of reality that does not change from day to day according to fashion or our mood or agenda. To change dharma into drama, all we need are the elements of any good play: emotion, conflict, and action—a sense that something urgent and meaningful is happening to the characters involved. Our personal dramas may begin with the "facts" about who we are and what we are doing, but fueled by our emotions and concepts, they can quickly evolve into pure imagination and become as difficult to decipher as the storylines of our dreams. Then our sense of reality becomes further and further removed from basic reality itself. We lose track of who we really are. We have no means of telling fact from fiction or developing the self-knowledge or wisdom that can free us from our illusions.

It took me a long time to see the differences between drama and dharma in my own life. Because they can look so much alike, they're hard to sort out, whether in Asian or Western culture. Looking back from my current life as a city dweller to my early childhood in a monastery, where I received intensive training to fill the role of Rinpoche to which

I was born, I realize that in certain respects these two lifestyles weren't that different. Then, as now, the dramas of life wove together with the dharma of life. In my youth, I had a number of daunting responsibilities. It was my job, for example, to take care of the business of spirituality—to perform ceremonial functions and uphold traditional cultural ways. However, I didn't always see the meaning in these activities or their connection to true wisdom. Though I was too young to understand those feelings, that slight disconnect started me off on an inquiry into what is real—and therefore genuinely meaningful—and what is only illusion. It was a dilemma for me, my personal drama, a first taste of rebellion that challenged my sense of identity and role as a future teacher in the tradition of my birth. Nevertheless, it also pushed me in the direction of dharma: my personal search for truth began right there, with questions, not answers.

REBEL WITHIN

In the summer of 1978, after being in the monastic educational system for eight years or so, I was studying the Vinaya literature, the Buddha's teachings on social science, governance, and ethical conduct intended primarily for the monastic community. While I was enjoying the feast of this wisdom and was genuinely inspired by it, I still noticed that little streak of rebelliousness coming up in me again—the same sense of dissatisfaction I had felt earlier with the empty rituals and institutionalized values of all religious traditions.

Later in my studies, I came across the Buddhist notion of emptiness and felt totally clueless. I wondered what the heck the Buddha was talking about: empty this, empty that; empty table, empty self. I could feel and see the table, and my good old sense of self was still intact. Nevertheless, as I contemplated these teachings, I realized that I had never explored my mind beyond my usual thought processes. I had never encountered certain deeper dimensions of my own mind. This emptiness, it turned out, was a revolutionary discovery, full of possibilities to free me from my lifelong blind faith in realism, which suddenly seemed so naïve and simpleminded. I felt so free just from reading these teachings, and that sense of freedom only increased with my wholehearted practice of them.

How wonderful it would be, I thought, if only we could practice the teachings of the Buddha as he really taught them from his own experience—free from the clouds of religiosity that often surround them. By themselves, they are powerful tools for intensifying awareness and triggering insight. Yet it's difficult to distinguish the tools themselves from their cultural packaging. When your friend gives you a gift, is the pretty paper that wraps that gift just paper—or part of the gift? Does the designer label on your shopping bag make the bag more valuable than the contents? Are the ceremonies and rituals of religious observance more important than what is being observed—the inexpressible sacredness of the truth of who we are?

It's not an easy thing to challenge your cultural conditioning, to break through its constraints, and then to go further and penetrate the more subtle conditioning of your own mind. But that's the nature of the search for truth that frees you from illusion. When I think of that freedom and finding the courage to break through the icy formalities of my own perfectionist Asian culture, I always recall the ancient Indian prince, Siddhartha, whose accomplishment still stands as a perfect example of a revolution of mind: a one-pointed search for the truth that led to his full awakening and freedom from all cultural and psychological bondage. He wanted nothing from the outside world. He was not on some emotional trip with an agenda of personal glorification and power. He simply wanted to know what was true and what was mere illusion. His sincerity and courage have always inspired me, and they can be an inspiration for anyone's search for truth and enlightenment.

This search is what *Rebel Buddha* is about. We all want to find some meaningful truth about who we are, and we're always looking for it. But we can only find it when we're guided by our own wisdom—our own rebel buddha within. With practice, we can sharpen our eyes and ears of wisdom, so that we will recognize the truth when we see it or hear it. But this kind of looking and listening is an art we must learn. So often, when we think we're being open and receptive, nothing is coming in. Our mind is already full of conclusions, judgments, or our own version of the facts. We're more intent on getting a stamp of approval for what we think we know than in learning something new. But when we're genuinely open-minded, what happens? There's a sense of space and invitation, a sense of inquisitiveness and of real connection with something beyond our usual selves. In that situation, we can hear whatever truth is speaking to us in the moment, whether the source is another person, a book, or our perceptions of the world itself. It's like listening to music. When you're totally into it, your mind goes to a different level. You're listening without judgment or intellectual interpretation because you're listening from the heart. That's how you need to listen when you want to hear the truth.

When you can feel the truth on that level, then you discover reality in its naked form, beyond culture, language, time, or location. That is the truth discovered by Siddhartha when he became the Buddha, or "Awakened One." Awakening to who we really are beyond our personal dramas and shifting cultural identities is a process of transforming illusion back into its basic state of reality. That transformation is the revolution of mind we are here to explore. After much thought about my own training, it is what I have tried to present here for modern readers: a culturally stripped-down vision of the Buddhist spiritual journey.

Beyond Culture

In my role as a teacher, my intention is simply to share the wisdom of the Buddha and my experiences in both traditional and contemporary settings of studying and practicing those teachings. In my teachings in recent years, I have also been trying to clarify frequent misunderstandings about Buddhism—especially the tendency to make Asian Buddhist culture stand for Buddhism itself—by pointing out the true essence of the teachings, which is wisdom joined with compassion. While not always easy to sort out, my various experiences have led me to see the almost blinding influence of culture in our lives and thus the importance of seeing beyond culture altogether. If we're ever to understand who we are as individuals and societies, then we need to see the interdependence of culture, identity, and meaning.

Since freedom is the goal of the Buddhist path, and wisdom is what we need to achieve that goal, it's important to ask ourselves, "What is real wisdom—knowledge that brings freedom and not bondage? How do we recognize it? How does it manifest in our lives and in the world? Does it have a cultural identity? Are the social and religious norms of everyday life an expression of true wisdom?" These questions inspired me to give a series of lectures on culture, values, and wisdom. It is from these lectures that the present book has been drawn.

To bring the wisdom of the Buddha from one culture and language into another is not an easy task. Simply having a good intention does not seem to be enough. Furthermore, the task is not simply one of direction, say from East to West. It is as much a movement through time as through physical space. It is one thing to visit a neighboring country with different customs and values and figure out how you can communicate with its people. You will find a way, because in spite of your differences, you share certain reference points and ways of thinking just by virtue of being contemporaries—of living together in the twenty-first century. But if you were transported two or three thousand years into the past or the future, you would have to find a way to connect with the mind of that age.

Similarly, we need to find a way to connect these ancient teachings on wisdom with our contemporary sensibilities. Only by stripping away irrelevant cultural and social values will we see the full spectrum of what this wisdom is in its naked form and what it has to offer our modern cultures. A true merging of this ancient wisdom with the psyche of the modern world can't take place as long as we're holding on tightly to the purely cultural habits and values of the East or West.

Like never before, the strict distinctions between East and West are dissolving in a world where globalization is bringing all of us the same problems and promises. From New Delhi to Toronto to San Antonio, we're talking to each other on Skype, sharing our stuff on Facebook, negotiating deals, watching the same silly YouTube videos, and drinking our Starbucks. We're also suffering the same panic attacks and depression, although I might take Valium and you might take Chinese herbs.

At the same time, every culture has its own unique set of eyes and ears by which it looks out on and interprets the world. We need to appreciate the impact of the psychology, history, and language of each society as it works to uphold a genuine Buddhist lineage of awakening on its home ground. It's one thing to welcome an interesting new spiritual tradition into our culture. It's another thing to keep it fresh and alive. When it starts to age, to become commonplace, we can become deaf and dumb to its message and power. Then it becomes like anything else to which we pay outward respect but little attention. When we lose our heart connection to anything, whether it's an old collection of comic books, a wedding ring, or the spiritual beliefs that will accompany us until the moment of our death, it becomes just part of the background noise of our life.

This is why, throughout the ages, Buddhism has had a history of revolution and renewal, of testing and challenging itself. If the tradition is not bringing awakening and freedom to those who practice it, then it is not being true to its philosophy or living up to its potential. There is no inherent awakening power in cultural forms that have become dissociated from the wisdom and practicality that gave birth to them. They turn into illusions themselves and become part of the drama of religious culture. Although they can make us happy temporarily, they can't free us from suffering, so at some point, they become a source of disappointment and discouragement. Eventually, these forms may inspire nothing more than resistance to their authority.

More Dharma, Less Drama

Growing up in a monastic institution in the Indian state of Sikkim, which was surrounded by ethnic Tibetan refugees, as well as tribal peoples of the Himalayan regions of India, Nepal, and Bhutan, I experienced both the richness and challenges of living in a diverse and multifaith culture. However, it was not until I came to New York City when I was fourteen, and then later studied at Columbia University in my twenties, that I really experienced a truly global multiculturalism and diversity of faith.

I think it was that first trip, when I had the good fortune of traveling with my own teacher, His Holiness the Sixteenth Karmapa, on a tour of the United States in 1980, that sealed my fate and led me to become the U.S. citizen I am today.

The cultural challenges I see in North America are not so different from those I find in Europe, Asia, or the Himalayan mountain communities where traditional Buddhist values are most closely preserved. Because of their power for good or ill in our lives, we need to look sincerely at our cultural traditions and the place we give them in our society. On the one hand, there are cultural forms that retain the wisdom of previous generations and function as important sources of knowledge for us. On the other hand, there are cultural forms that don't retain any of the wisdom they may once have held and that are utterly lacking in compassion. From the notion of untouchable castes in India, to the feudalistic rule of nineteenth-century Tibet, to the burning of witches in Europe and the slavery of Africans in America, painful and unjust practices devoid of sense or wisdom survived unchallenged for too long. When our thoughts and actions are dictated by powerful pressures from unreasonable social, religious, or cultural values, we can become stuck in a joyless place where we know nothing but suffering and further bondage. True wisdom is free of the dramas of culture or religion and should bring us only a sense of peace and happiness.

However, we're often addicted to our dramas and fearful of the truth. If you want to see real drama, you don't need to turn on your TV—it's right there in your life, which is full of emotions, anxiety, and depression. And if you want to gossip about drama, you don't need to go to a chat room. It's happening right there in your thoughts. Even in this day and age, when we have so many material resources, comforts, and entertainments and distractions available 24/7, we find that we can't get through the day without feeling a little bit depressed, and we don't know how to enjoy ourselves without feeling guilty. Even when we have an almost perfect day, we find ourselves asking, "Do I really deserve this? Did I work hard enough to earn it?" Wherever there is ego-centered drama, there is suffering. It goes on and on until we see beyond this drama to the dharma of our true selves.

Nothing Happens

When I was studying at Columbia University and my teachers asked me to introduce myself to my classmates, I was speechless. I wasn't sure who I really was. Was I Tibetan simply because of my parents, or was I Indian because I was born on that continent? Or was I neither—a stateless person without any citizenship? Having immigrated first to Canada and then to the United States, now when I go back to India for visits, everything seems a little foreign to me. My conversations with friends and former colleagues are different. We don't always share the same sense of humor or everyday references anymore, and our values seem to be shifting. Here I go again; I am a foreigner in my own birth country and a stranger to my old friends. While it's not surprising that I'd feel like a stranger at a county fair in the midwestern United States, it is surprising to feel like an alien in the place where I grew up. Now the only places I feel unnoticed and normal are on the subways and streets of New York City; in my first home in North America, downtown Vancouver; or in my Seattle basement apartment, where my day begins with a cup of coffee and ends with the Colbert Report in the evening. Who am I now, really? And what has happened to me? As the Sixteenth Karmapa once said, "Nothing happens," so perhaps nothing has really happened to me. The fact is I am a Generation Xer, according to some, and a loyal BlackBerry subject, but the truth is I am a rebel without any culture on my way to finding the buddha I know is within me.

My intention in sharing this journey of mind and its culture, here and in the following pages, is to echo the Buddha's message that the truth about who we really are, beyond all appearances, is knowledge worth seeking. It leads to freedom, and freedom to happiness. May everyone enjoy perfect happiness, and may that happiness, in turn, liberate the suffering of the world.

rebel buddha

WHEN YOU HEAR the word *buddha*, what do you think of? A golden statue? A young prince seated under a spreading tree? Or maybe Keanu Reeves in the movie *Little Buddha*? Robed monks, shaved heads? You may have many associations or none at all. Most of us are far removed from any realistic connection to the word.

The word *buddha*, however, simply means "awake" or "awakened." It does not refer to a particular historical person or to a philosophy or religion. It refers to your own mind. You know you have a mind, but what's it like? It's awake. I don't just mean "not asleep." I mean your mind is *really* awake, beyond your imagination. Your mind is brilliantly clear, open, spacious, and full of excellent qualities: unconditional love, compassion, and wisdom that sees things as they truly are. In other words, your awakened mind is always a good mind; it's never dull or confused. It's never distressed by the doubts, fears, and emotions that so often torture us. Instead, your true mind is a mind of joy, free from all suffering. That is who you really are. That is the true nature of your mind and the mind of everyone. But your mind doesn't just sit there being perfect, doing nothing. It's at play all the time, creating your world.

If this is true, then why isn't your life, and the whole world, perfect? Why aren't you happy all the time? How could you be laughing one minute and in despair the next? And why would "awakened" people argue, fight, lie, cheat, steal, and go to war? The reason is that, even though the awakened state is the true nature of the mind, most of us don't see it. Why? Something is in the way. Something is blocking our view of it. Sure, we see bits of it here and there. But the moment we see it, something else pops into our mind—"What time is it? Is it time for lunch? Oh, look, a butterfly!"—and our insight is gone.

Ironically, what blocks your view of your mind's true nature—your buddha mind—is also your own mind, the part of your mind that is always busy, constantly involved in a steady stream of thoughts, emotions, and concepts. This busy mind is who you think you are. It is easier to see, like the face of the person standing right in front of you. For example, the thought you're thinking right now is more obvious to you than your awareness of that thought. When you get angry, you pay more attention to what you're angry about than to the actual source of your anger, where your anger is coming from. In other words, you notice what your mind is doing, but you don't see the mind itself. You identify yourself with the contents of this busy mind—your thoughts, emotions, ideas—and end up thinking that all of this stuff is "me" and "how I am."

When you do that, it's like being asleep and dreaming and believing that your dream images are true. If, for example, you dream that you're being chased by a menacing stranger, it's very scary and real. However, as soon as you wake up, both the stranger and your feelings of terror are simply gone, and you feel great relief. Furthermore, if you had known you were dreaming in the first place, then you wouldn't have experienced any fear.

In a similar way, in our ordinary life, we're like dreamers believing that the dream we're having is real. We think we're awake, but we're not. We think that this busy mind of thoughts and emotions is who we truly are. But when we actually wake up, our misunderstanding about who we are—and the suffering that confusion brings—is gone.

A Rebel Within

If we could, we would probably all sink completely into this dream that passes for our waking life, but something keeps rousing us from our sleep. No matter how dazed and confused it gets, our drowsy self is always linked to complete wakefulness. That wakefulness has a sharp and penetrating quality. It's our own intelligence and clear awareness that have the ability to see through whatever blocks our view of our true self—the true nature of our mind. On the one hand, we're used to our sleep and content with its dreams; on the other hand, our wakeful self is always shaking us up and turning on the lights, so to speak. This wakeful self, the true mind that is awake, wants out of the confines of sleep, out of illusion-like reality. While we're locked away in our dream, it sees the potential for freedom. So it provokes, arouses, prods, and instigates until we're inspired to take action. You could say we are living with a rebel within.

When we think of political or social rebels—historical or contemporary, well-known or forgotten—people who fought and are fighting for the cause of liberty and justice, we think of them as heroes: from the fathers of the American Revolution to Harriet Tubman; Mohandas Gandhi; Martin Luther King, Jr.; Aung San Suu Kyi; and Nelson Mandela. Today, we stand in awe of their courage, compassion, and remarkable achievements. Yet such idealists and reformers are always regarded as troublemakers by those they challenge. Their ideas and intentions, and even their company, are not always welcome. Rebels are a mixed blessing it seems—good for the movie business, but in real life, they make people nervous. They're hard to push aside. They keep coming back with questions no one else will ask. They won't settle for partial truths or uncertain answers. They refuse to follow conventions that control or imprison them or the people of their society. Their path to victory runs through some rough territory. But their rebel character is not easily discouraged. Commitment to a cause—a greater vision of what might be—is the rebel's lifeblood.

On the spiritual path, this rebel is the voice of your own awakened mind. It is the sharp, clear intelligence that resists the status quo of your confusion and suffering. What is this rebel buddha like? A troublemaker of heroic proportions. Rebel buddha is the renegade that gets you to switch your allegiance from sleep to the awakened state. This means you have the power to wake up your dreaming self, the imposter that is pretending to be the real you. You have the means to break loose from whatever binds you to suffering and locks you in confusion. You are the champion of your own freedom. Ultimately, the mission of rebel buddha is to instigate a revolution of mind.

ORDINARY BUDDHAS

This book is about a path to freedom described by the historical buddha, Buddha Shakyamuni, twenty-six hundred years ago. There are many beautiful and eloquent stories about the Buddha's birth, his life, and how he reached the state of enlightenment. Some treat the Buddha as an ordinary man who lived an exceptional life. Others consider him a kind of spiritual Superman, a divine being whose actions showed how ordinary people could achieve the same freedom he had found.

Actually, the basic elements of the Buddha's early life are not so different from our own, except for the fact that he came from a wealthy, royal family and most of us don't. At heart, however, what we see when we look at Buddha Shakyamuni's early life—when he was known simply as Siddhartha—is a young man's struggle for independence and freedom against the authority of his parents and society. On one level, it's a classic tale of the rich kid who runs away from home:

> Siddhartha, the future Buddha, was born the only son of the king and queen of the Shakyas, a kingdom in northern India. He lived a protected and luxurious life, closely controlled by his parents, who awaited the day the young prince would succeed his father to the throne. He had every advantage, privilege, and enjoyment you could imagine—the fabulous palace, designer clothes, servants, and grand parties with celebrities and lobbyists. But in the end, Siddhartha wasn't content with a life of just material possessions, social status, and political power. He longed to discover life's meaning and purpose in the face of what awaits us all: sickness, old age, and death. He struggled for a while to fulfill his parents' wishes but finally decided he had to go his own way. In the dead of night, he deserted the palace alone, trading his comfort and protection for the unknown, a destiny he hadn't yet discovered.

If we moved this ancient tale to New York City today, we'd have a modern American story:

A wealthy and prominent couple were expecting their first child. Understanding the dangers and difficulties of the modern world, they vowed to use their wealth and connections to make their child's life as safe and easy as possible. Even before he was born, he was enrolled in the most exclusive preschool. The child was given a long, illustrious name that echoed the greatness of his family lineage, but his friends all called him Sid. He grew up within the circle of the social and political elite of New York, enjoying every advantage. His parents envisioned a special destiny for him and even imagined his marriage to the daughter of the senator from . . .

We wouldn't be surprised to learn that Sid eventually decides to join a rock band, go backpacking in Alaska, or just stick his thumb out on the road to see where life takes him. The same holds true for any young person or youthful heart. Whatever our situation, ordinary or extraordinary, we want to discover our own path. We want to find the ultimate meaning of our life.

We know from history that Prince Siddhartha was successful in his quest, but we don't really know about our modern-day friend, Sid. We'll wish him the best. The point here is that, at the moment of their departure, neither one of them knows what the future holds. Both are taking a profound risk, abandoning security and the known world for a leap into the unknown. But it is as natural for Sid to take that risk as it was for Siddhartha to leap the palace fence. The impulse toward freedom is an essential part of our makeup; it is not the exclusive domain of special beings or men in robes from long ago or faraway lands. This desire for freedom is quite ordinary. In fact, "freedom-loving" is a common description of the American character—at least that's what you hear on the news—but take a walk on the streets of any modern city, and you will find the same spirit, especially among the young.

The very youth of America no doubt contributes to this freedom-loving nature. Other than the indigenous peoples of North America, most everyone here now is a recent arrival from Europe or Asia or Africa. While most of us today are somewhat removed from our ethnic roots, and some may have forgotten them entirely (and believe simply that "I'm an American"), in some sense, what is best and most unique about America is just this global ancestry, pioneering spirit, and independence of character to which all the world seems to have contributed.

This melting pot of America is home to trailblazers, inventors, free-thinkers, and visionaries, as well as pragmatists and puritans. Avant-garde artists and musicians ride the subways alongside corporate bankers and factory workers. Everyone is officially welcome. America's family gatherings are full of sparks—from those at your house to those played out on the national stage and documented by CNN and *Entertainment Weekly*. But when the sparks from this rubbing together of opposites ignite in an atmosphere of openness, it makes all the difference. Then, instead of pure friction, we get a lively dance that generates a very creative energy. By testing limits, pushing the envelope of old concepts, what was once unthinkable becomes the new norm. For example, not so long ago, no one had ever dreamed of flipping a switch and having a light go on, much less of watching faraway images on TV or surfing in cyberspace. Even as recently as the 1960s, we were amazed as we watched a man walking on the moon from our living room, which suddenly seemed quite small.

Getting Where We're Going

Just as scientists are constantly striving to unlock the secrets of the external world to discover the nature of reality, Siddhartha dreamed of unlocking the secrets of the inner world of the mind. When he left the palace, he left behind a young wife, a child, and his life of luxury. He was determined to conquer his ignorance and meet reality face-to-face. He went into the forest with no guarantee of a roof over his head, no means of sustenance, and no one to protect him.

At that time, Indian society was at an interesting point. The social structure was very rigid. A caste system decided your place in society, your duty in life, your occupation, and your spiritual standing. All this was set up by the condition of your birth. On the other hand, it was also a time of intense excitement. Intellectuals and philosophers were persistently engaged in lively debates that produced a number of competing spiritual traditions. Groups of young people began hanging out in the forest, joining one or another of these groups, which existed outside of society. Siddhartha, too, joined in, studying with two of the most renowned forest sages. As it happened, he quickly outstripped his teachers' understanding and then joined a group of five ascetic practitioners. More determined than ever to reach his goal, he abandoned all comfort. He took on the torturous practices of the ascetics, including starvation, with the intention of transcending the physical body and exhausting the desires of the mind. After six years of this, Siddhartha was near death. At that point, he let go of his belief that this path of intense deprivation would lead him to freedom. He collapsed by the bank of a river.

Though he didn't know it, Siddhartha was very near his goal. A young girl carrying a bowl of rice milk was passing by and offered him this food. He accepted it, breaking his six-year fast. Seeing this, his five ascetic brothers thought Siddhartha had given up his discipline. Furious, they vowed never to speak to him again and left. Siddhartha contemplated his situation while gradually regaining his strength. He realized that neither his life of self-indulgence in the palace nor his life of self-mortification in the forest was a genuine road to freedom. They were both extreme paths, and attachment to either extreme was an obstacle. The true way lay in the middle of these two. Recognizing this, he was ready for the final push. He sat on a grass cushion beneath the sheltering branches of a tree and took a personal vow to remain there until he knew the truth about his mind and the world.

Siddhartha meditated for forty-nine days, and at the age of thirty-five, he attained the freedom he sought. His mind became vast and open. He saw the truth of the suffering of all beings and the cause of that suffering. He saw that freedom is a reality within the reach of all beings, and he saw how they could attain it. He became known as the Buddha, the Awakened One, and he taught whoever came to him for the next forty-five years. Others followed his instructions. They attained their own freedom, and a lineage of awakening had begun.

what you should know

Since we're talking about the Buddhist spiritual path as a road to freedom, we need to ask, "Freedom from what? And what does this freedom look like?" In other words, we need to find out what the Buddha says about the starting point and end point of this journey. Then we can look into that and see if it holds up under scrutiny, and if it is the right path for us.

Sometimes we think that freedom means simply being free of any outside control—we can do whatever we like, when we like. Or maybe we think it means we're not controlled by inner psychological forces that inhibit the free expression of our feelings. But these kinds of freedom are only partial. If they aren't accompanied by intelligence and basic good sense, we could end up just acting impulsively, letting our emotions off the leash. We might be free to shout at people or stay out all night indulging our appetite for excitement and sensation, but we're certainly not in charge, and we're not free. We may feel temporarily energized and liberated by that kind of freedom, but the feeling is short-lived and usually followed by more pain and more confusion. We may also think that freedom means having a choice. We are free to choose what to do with our life, our time, and our money. We may choose wisely or foolishly, but it's our choice.

This so-called freedom, however, is just a façade when we make the same choices every day, do the same things over and over and react in the same ways. Whether we're free spirits or traditionalists, type A or type B personalities, our actions are equally predictable. When we look beneath the surface to see what's going on, why we're unhappy, we see the same storyline repeated again and again. If we fight with our boss at work, we probably fight at home with our partner or our kids. We struggle here and there in our life with the same unconscious patterns of aggression, desire, jealousy, or denial, until we're caught in a web of our own making. These are precisely the things from which we work to free ourselves on the Buddhist path: the habitual patterns that dominate our life and make it hard to see the awakened state of mind.

If you're interested in "meeting the Buddha" and following the spiritual path he described, then there are a few things you should know before you begin. First, Buddhism is primarily a study of mind and a system for training the mind. It is spiritual in nature, not religious. Its goal is self-knowledge, not salvation; freedom, not heaven. It relies on reason and analysis, contemplation and meditation, to transform knowledge about something into knowledge that surpasses understanding. But without your curiosity and questions, there is no path, no journey to be taken, even if you adopt all the forms of the tradition.

When Siddhartha left the palace to search for enlightenment, he didn't leave because he had such strong faith in a particular religion, had met a charismatic guru, or had received a calling from God. He didn't leave because he was exchanging one belief system for another, like a Christian who becomes a Hindu or a Republican who becomes a Democrat. His journey began simply with his desire to know the truth about life's meaning and purpose. He was searching for something without knowing what he was seeking.

What Are We Looking For?

Why do any of us enter a spiritual path today? What are we looking for? Whether our problem is suffering or a desire "to know," we're living with profound questions every day. Why do you get out of bed when the alarm goes off at 6:30 A.M.? What goes through your mind when you turn out the light at midnight? Our questions get lost in the busyness of our life, but they never really go away. If we can catch them and look at them in odd moments—when we're pouring our first cup of coffee or waiting at a red light—we can begin to see beyond this "job of life" to life itself. We don't have to wait until life becomes shaky—until we're facing the pain of depression, disappointment, loss, or the fear of death—to ask questions that are "spiritual" in nature. All we need to do is let our questions back in. Tell them, "You're important to me now."

To discover your real questions, simply take a time-out. Stop looking ahead of yourself at where you're going or backward at where you've been. When you do stop, there's a sense of going nowhere. There's a sense of gap, which is a tremendous relief. You can simply breathe and be who you are. At the same time, there is a basic sense of "what?" Maybe that's your first real question. Just be there with that "what?" with an open mind. That "what?" is like an open door. Something will come through it. It may be an answer or another question. You don't have to do anything but be there to meet it.

In the beginning, we may think that having questions is a sign of ignorance. The more questions we have, the more we don't know. The more answers we have, the wiser we are. However, knowing clearly what you don't know is already a form of wisdom. Real ignorance is not knowing what you don't know. When you think you know something you don't, it can lead to a kind of make-believe wisdom, an imaginary sense of knowledge that is powerless to free you from your confusion.

As long as our questions are sincere and honest, not questions that will make us feel smart or look better, the questioning mind opens up the spiritual journey. But we must learn to work with our questions skillfully. We're going through a process that takes time and necessarily brings up doubt and skepticism. If we merely accept everything that's thrown at us, then where has our intelligence gone? We actually need intelligent doubt and skepticism; they protect us against mistaken views and propaganda. A healthy dose of doubt and skepticism will lead us to precise and clear questions. Doubt only becomes negative when it continues on and on, never finding its end. If we never get beyond our uncertainty to a sense of understanding, then we can start to feel a little crazy or paranoid. Doubt that leads us to authentic knowledge and confidence turns out to be wisdom in the end.

What Are We Doing Here?

On this path, we're searching for meaningful knowledge: we want to know who we are and why things happen to us. We also want to understand our relationship to the world and why things happen to others. Even if we're not so concerned on our own behalf, we might care a great deal when it comes to someone else—an innocent child mistreated, a friend in crisis, a village wiped out by nature, a species wiped out by mankind. Aside from managing to survive until we're put in a nursing home by our children, what are we doing here? You can contemplate such large questions for inspiration, but it's best to start where you are. Stay close to home, to your mind, your body, your life. If you can discover a meaningful question right here, it will probably apply to someone else as well—and maybe to the motion of the planets. You never know.

A spiritual question is primarily one we ask ourselves and process alone. Just as our answers must come from within, our questions come from inside us too. They come from the same place. All our questions are connected to something we already know. Each question will lead to an answer that will lead to further questions and so on. As our understanding grows, our questions become clearer and our answers more meaningful. This is how the spiritual path progresses.

At some point, you'll be certain that you have reached a full understanding of your question. You'll recognize it because it's not someone else's answer—it's your own. You should keep questioning until you reach that point. How can you tell if you've stopped searching before you've reached that kind of certainty? One sign is when you look to someone else for answers to your questions. That brings your search to a halt. At that point, your inquisitive mind is no longer working.

It's true that others can help us, but that doesn't mean there is someone out there who can give us all the answers. We can rely on the teachings of the Buddha and on spiritual friends to some degree. Knowledge that comes from sources we respect can help us clarify and refine our understanding. But that doesn't mean that we fully accept what anyone says and give up our search, or that once we've heard from someone we consider to be an authority, it's the end of the matter. Their discovery and understanding of the truth doesn't help us if we don't really connect with them. If their experience doesn't agree with our own, then it's of no use to us, regardless of how profound a truth it is for them.

Eventually, you'll arrive at some form of final question—a sense of uncertainty or doubt that stays with you for a while. By the time you arrive at that clear question, you'll already have made a considerable journey. You'll already have answered hundreds or thousands of other questions in order to get there. Having a clear question means you know clearly what it is that you don't know. Now you have a question that you can take to your teachers or look up in books. On the other hand, if you ask a teacher a question that isn't clear to you, then nothing he or she says can help you. There can be no clear answer to a half-baked question. On the other hand, if you're simply looking for answers, any answer, then you'll find thousands of books—Buddhist books, Christian books, New Age books, and what have you—that answer all kinds of questions. But none of the facts in those books can enlighten you if your question is vague.

The wisdom we're looking for is not just an answer we get from a religious person or subject matter expert who tells us what to think. Real wisdom is when you find a true question. When you find it, you should not rush to answer it. Stay with it for a while. Make friends with it. We live in "instant times"—instant messaging, instant pictures, fast food—and our mind is accustomed these days to instant gratification. If we bring this expectation to our spiritual path, however, we'll be disappointed. Some of our questions can't be answered right away. We must be as patient as scientists are when they run their experiments and diligently evaluate and verify their findings.

A Scientific Approach

We often mix together spirituality and religion as if they were one thing. But this doesn't quite work. A spiritual path can exist within or outside a religious context. Religion and spirituality can be complementary or separate practices and experiences. A spiritual path is an inner journey that begins with questions about who we are, and about the nature and meaning of our existence. It's naturally a process of introspection and contemplation.

Religion, as conventionally defined, refers to a set of beliefs about the cause and nature of the universe, our relationship to the creation and creator, and the source of spiritual authority. We can accept those beliefs at face value or explore and examine our own experience of them. Some religions embrace such questioning, while others discourage it, either openly or implicitly. The point is, we need to be clear about what we're really doing in our spiritual or religious life.

Although Buddhism can be practiced "religiously," in many respects, it isn't really a religion. Because of its emphasis on questioning and working with the mind, it is spiritual in nature. But because it relies on logical analysis and reasoning, as well as on meditation, many Buddhist teachers regard Buddhism as a science of mind rather than a religion. In each meditation session, we gather knowledge about the mind through observation, questioning, and testing. We do this over and over, until we gradually develop a meaningful understanding of our own mind. Some people may even become weary of Buddhism because it gives them so much work to do—they have to ask all the questions and find all their own answers.

The alternative to taking on this responsibility is to let religion do the job for us. We can give up just a little of our critical intelligence by not asking too many questions, which is what most of us do. Or we can go all the way, give up all our questions, and become religious fundamentalists of one sort or another. Then we are relieved from all worries about what to think and why.

In whatever way we label the teachings of the Buddha—as a religion or spiritual path—the body of knowledge that comprises the Buddhist scriptures is not intended to be a substitute for your own questioning process. It's more like a well-equipped research laboratory where you can find tools of all kinds to investigate your own experience. In fact, some Buddhist views would be regarded as antireligious in some quarters. First, it is a nontheistic tradition. From Buddhism's point of view, there is no supernatural entity outside of our own mind. There is no being or force that has the power to control our experience or create a heaven or hell of it. That capability resides only in the power of our mind. Even enlightened beings like the Buddha don't have the power to control the minds of others. They can't create a better or worse world for us or undo our confusion. Our confusion is created by our own mind, and it can only be transformed by our mind. So the most powerful entity in the Buddhist spiritual path is the mind.

The closest thing to the notion of a god in Buddhism is probably the state of enlightenment. But even enlightenment is regarded as a human accomplishment: the development of consciousness to its highest state. The Buddha taught that every human being has the capacity to achieve that level of realization. That's the difference in the approaches of nontheistic and theistic traditions. If I said, "I want to become God," it would sound crazy or even blasphemous to a theist. It would be considered a very ambitious, very ego-centered thought. But in the Buddhist tradition, we're encouraged to become like Buddha—awakened ones.

The Buddha also taught another somewhat challenging idea: the notion of emptiness. We will take this up later, but for the moment, we can simply say it's the view that there is no real self and no real world that exists in exactly the way it appears to us now. The Buddha said that when we don't comprehend emptiness, we don't see what's really there—we see only a coarse version of reality. So from the Buddhist point of view, there is not only no savior, there is also no one to be saved.

However shocking or radical this sounds, it's not much different from what science is currently telling us about the subatomic world. Thanks to scientific research, we now know that the world we perceive with our naked eyes is something of an optical illusion. Beneath its solid surface, something else entirely is going on. If you try to find the real stuff of matter, all you'll find is particles acting like waves and waves acting like particles, and where any of this is located at any particular moment is pure guesswork. In the view of this cutting-edge scientific knowledge, not only are matter and energy interchangeable, but there may also be multiple dimensions of something called "space-time."

When you hear things like this about the universe from a scientist, it sounds fascinating and very spiritual. But when you hear something similar about yourself from the Buddha, the idea of an almighty god and a literal heaven might start to sound very appealing. However, what initially scares us about emptiness turns out to be good news. When we look at emptiness more closely, we see that it's actually full. *Emptiness* is simply a word that describes an experience; our mind then takes that word and makes it into a concept. If we take the concept to be the actual experience, then we miss the best part. If you had never experienced love, for example, and all you knew about it was the dictionary definition, then you'd certainly be missing the fullness of that experience. It's the same with emptiness. In fact, emptiness and love are related. We'll get to this later too. For now, let's just say that when you unite the two, you have an experience that is beyond either one. The experience of this union of love and emptiness is the awakening of your own rebel buddha heart.

THINGS AS THEY ARE

We're always trying to catch up with reality, which just "is." Whether we love it or hate it, or love or hate each other, we can't change the way things are at their deepest levels. We can't stop being who we truly are, just as we can't stop a subatomic particle from being what it truly is, even if it's contrary to our concepts about it. The makeup of the physical world is constantly being reexamined and reenvisioned. When we bring these views to bear on the world we take to be so solid, we're getting closer to what the Buddha taught twenty-six hundred years ago about the ultimate unreality and unfindability of all phenomena.

In Buddhism, we aren't trying to look at the physical world by itself; instead, we're looking at the mind and its relationship to the appearances of the world. We observe the mind to see what the mind itself is and how it acts in relation to our internal and external experiences of everything—from thoughts and emotions to actual things. To do this, we need a special set of tools that can take us beyond the mind's limitations. Buddhism uses the tools of meditation and a process of reasoning.

We need to ask ourselves in the beginning, "Am I willing to let go of my attachment to what I believe in order to see something new? Am I open to the possibility of an inconceivable reality?" Our main problem is that such a reality doesn't fit in with our ordinary experience. If we believe that our senses and our conceptual mind are giving us a true and complete picture of the world and who we are in it, we're just fooling ourselves. We need to expand our understanding beyond our sense perceptions and concepts, which are nothing but tiny windows through which we see only a partial reality. In order to see a higher level of reality, we need to look out of a larger window. In Buddhism, intellectual analysis on the one hand and opening up to what lies beyond concept on the other are not regarded as contradictory. When we're able to think critically and at the same time be open to experiences that lie beyond what we know, then we start seeing the big picture.

From this, we can see that the Buddhist spiritual path does not fit neatly into the category or general understanding of religion, except perhaps in an academic sense. You can practice Buddhism as a traditional religion, if that's what suits you. There are Buddhist churches that provide a sense of community for their members and a regular schedule of social activities and meditation practice. The values of harmonious, compassionate living are cultivated, and there's a sense of reverence for the Buddha and the great teachers who came after him. This is a valuable aspect of the tradition as well, and it's the way Buddhism is practiced in many places around the world. However, the essence of Buddhism transcends all these forms. It is the pure wisdom and compassion that exists in inconceivable measure within the minds of all beings, and the Buddhist spiritual path is the journey we take to fully realize this true nature of mind.

BLIND FAITH

As modern, rational people living in the scientific age, we like to think that our beliefs are based on things like experience, good judgment, and reasoning rather than blind faith. Blind faith applies to children or people who are more innocent and naïve about the world. But if we honestly examine our ordinary assumptions, we find that many of our beliefs are simply things we've been told, things we take for granted. Believing without understanding is the meaning of blind faith. This kind of blind faith shows up in the common knowledge we live by every day.

We assume that things are what they are because everybody says so. From the time we learned to speak as kids, we discovered that everything has a name, and that name is what a thing is. We don't question it. We also don't see the power of those labels to shape our thinking or limit our understanding. When we call a table "a table," a couple of things are happening. We know where to sit to eat dinner or set up our computer. At the same time, we're assuming—without ever thinking about it—that something called "table" truly exists. So naming and labeling always function on multiple levels. They help us live together in the world (a definite plus), and they also make our world heavier and more solid.

Our blind faith in our mundane reality is no different from religious blind faith: someone tells you that heaven and hell exist, and consequently you fix your hopes on one and live in fear of the other. But what do "heaven" and "hell" really mean? Where are they? What act will push you across the line into one or the other? If you die at the age of eighteen or eighty, will you be forever young or forever old in heaven? Buddha's advice to us is to challenge our blind faith wherever it manifests. In order to find out what's really going on at any level of reality, we have to approach our experience with discriminating awareness. Remember, at one time everyone thought the world was flat and the sun circled around it.

Ironically, in some respects, modern science has become our collective religion. We tend to believe what science tells us about our physical reality without much thought. On the other hand, when we're told about the true nature of mind, we don't easily believe it. Why do we believe in black holes, something we can't readily experience, but doubt that our mind is awakened? While we may not have the opportunity to personally verify the research of scientists, we can evaluate the Buddha's teachings on mind firsthand. At some point, after a period of questioning, analysis, and meditation, we can say with certainty whether those teachings are true in our experience or not.

One of the most important teachings given by the Buddha is a simple, commonsense statement that carries profound implications for both our social and spiritual lives. In answer to a question posed by villagers about how to know what to believe when there are so many conflicting belief systems and doctrines being asserted by passing teachers and pundits, the Buddha once advised,

> Do not believe in anything simply because you have heard it.
> Do not believe in anything because it is spoken and rumored by many.
> Do not believe in anything simply because it is found written in your religious books.
> Do not believe in anything merely on the authority of your teachers and elders.
> Do not believe in traditions because they have been handed down for many generations.
> But after observation and analysis, when you find that anything agrees with reason and is conducive to the good and benefit of one and all, then accept it and live up to it.[1]

What the Buddha is saying in this quotation is that we must investigate any presentation of the truth that claims to be authoritative. We should question its reasoning and logic with our own reasoning and logic. We should analyze it from top to bottom, inside and out. If we find that it's reasonable, helpful, and beneficial not just for ourselves but for others as well, then we can accept it. The Buddha actually says, ". . . then accept it and *live up to it.*" This is an important teaching for us, because it's possible—in fact, it's common—to hear a profound teaching on compassion or emptiness or to read a scientific proof of global warming and accept it, but not live by its implications. We're so enthusiastic at first, but there is no follow-through. This is because we haven't examined it to such an extent that we really know what it means. As long as our understanding is vague, we're doubtful. So if there is any wisdom there, it never touches us in a meaningful way.

Ultimately, the Buddha is saying that the solution to our doubts is not to adopt the blind faith of "true believers"—even, or especially, Buddhist true believers. Instead, it's an unshakable certainty, a complete trust in our own hard-won understanding about the nature of things. We trust this understanding because we've arrived at it through our own investigation. From this perspective, we can say that genuine faith is simply confidence and trust in ourselves, in our own intelligence and understanding, which then extends to the path we're traveling. But we need to find our own way, because there is no "one-size-fits-all" spiritual path. We find that path through examination and questioning, and through our genuine heart of inquisitiveness. We can rely on the wisdom of the Buddha as an example, but to understand that wisdom for ourselves, we must rely on our own rebel buddha mind.

getting to know your mind

ALL THE TEACHINGS of the Buddha have one clear message, which is that there is nothing more important than getting to know your own mind. The reason is simple—the source of our every suffering is discovered within this mind. If we're feeling anxious, that stress and worry are produced by this mind. If we're overwrought by despair, that misery originates within our mind. On the other hand, if we're madly in love and walking on air, that joy also arises from our mind. Pleasure and pain, simple and extreme, are experiences of mind. Mind is the experiencer of each moment of our life and all that we perceive, think, and feel. Therefore, the better we know our mind and how it works, the greater the possibility that we can free ourselves from the mental states that weigh us down, invisibly wound us, and destroy our ability to be happy. Knowing our mind not only leads to a happy life, it transforms every trace of confusion and wakes us up completely.

To experience that awakened state is to know freedom in its purest sense. This state of freedom is not dependent on external circumstances. It does not change with the ups and downs of life. It's the same whether we experience gain or loss, praise or blame, pleasant or unpleasant conditions. In the beginning, we only glimpse this state, but those glimpses become increasingly more familiar and stable. In the end, the state of freedom becomes our home ground.

THE MIND AS A STRANGER

Perhaps there's a stranger you see every day in your neighborhood. Maybe this person's face or way of walking or dressing is familiar to you because you've passed him so many times on the street. But you've never exchanged more than a nod or a polite hello. You've never struck up a conversation because you're fearful about approaching someone unknown. You don't know if this person is sane or crazy—someone who is kind, loving, and potentially a good friend, or a menace to society. Since you're busy anyway, and there is no urgency to find out, you let it go and continue on your way. But the next day, you see this person again, and again the day after that. Eventually, some kind of connection takes place.

In many ways, our mind is like the stranger we see on the streets of our neighborhood. We might protest, "But how can this be, when I am with my mind all the time?" To say that our own mind is a stranger seems absurd. The problem, for most of us, is that our acquaintance with our mind doesn't go much past saying hello. We may have said hello so many times that we feel we're old friends, but how well do we really know our mind? It's more likely that our relationship with our mind is a distant one—not an intimate friendship—because we haven't spent much meaningful time together. We're aware of its presence, its general features, and even its changeability. But we don't know its full story; we don't really know what makes it tick. We may have noticed that sometimes it behaves very pleasantly and reasonably, and other times it starts kicking and screaming. So we remain on guard; we're not sure whether this stranger that's the mind will turn out to be a great companion or suddenly turn on us like the shadowy figures in our nightmares. We're curious, but from a safe distance.

So what is this mysterious stranger called "the mind"? Is mind the brain or a by-product of the brain? Is it chemicals and neurotransmitters lighting up pathways in the brain that spark sensation, thought, and feeling, and lead up to the brilliance of consciousness? That's basically the materialist view of neuroscience, which sees mind as a function of the brain. From a Buddhist point of view, however, mind and body are separate entities. While the brain and its functions undoubtedly do give rise to certain coarse levels of mental phenomena, mind in its more subtle and ultimate sense is not material or necessarily tied to any physical base.

Two Aspects of the Mind

As we've seen already, Buddhism talks about mind in different ways. There is the mind that is confused or asleep and the mind that is enlightened or awake. Another way to describe the mind is to talk about its relative and ultimate aspects. The relative aspect refers to confused mind; the ultimate aspect is its enlightened nature. Relative mind is our ordinary consciousness, our commonplace dualistic perception of the world. "I" am separate from "you," and "this" is separate from "that." There appears to be a fundamental division within all of our experiences. We take for granted that good exists apart from bad, right apart from wrong, and so forth. This way of seeing tends to breed misunderstanding and conflict more often than harmony. The ultimate aspect of mind is simply the true nature of our mind, which is beyond any polarities. It is our fundamental being, our basic, open, and spacious awareness. Imagine a clear blue sky filled with light.

Day-to-Day Mind

Relative mind is our day-to-day mind of perceptions, thoughts, and emotions. We could also call it our moment-to-moment mind, because it moves and changes at such high speed—now seeing, now hearing, now thinking, now feeling, and so on. Actually, it's three minds rolled into one: perceptual mind, conceptual mind, and emotional mind. Together, these three layers or aspects of relative mind account for all of our conscious mental activity. It's important to understand how they work together to create all the kinds of experiences we go through.

First, perceptual mind refers to our direct perceptions of sight, sound, smell, taste, and touch. Because they arise and pass so quickly, we usually don't pay much attention to these experiences; we miss them and jump straight into the second aspect of mind, conceptual, or thinking, mind. The exception might be when we're so tired that we sit without a thought in our head and begin to notice the colors of the leaves on the trees, the sounds of birds, the ripples on a lake—in other words, we have a simple, direct perception of the world. But usually, our mind is too busy to notice our perceptions. They go by too fast.

For example, if there is a table in front of us, by the time we notice it, what we're seeing is just our thought, "Oh, it's a table." We aren't seeing the actual table anymore; we're seeing the label *table*, which is an abstraction. An abstraction is both a mental construct—an idea we form quickly based on a perception—and a generalization that's one step removed from our direct experience. It lacks the experience of genuine contact, which yields more information as well as a greater sense of pleasure or satisfaction. We continually produce one label after another, unaware of how far removed we are from our own experience, and this is what we call conceptual mind. Our concepts then become triggers for the third level of mind, which is emotional mind. We react to these labels and get caught up in our habitual feelings of like and dislike, jealousy, anger, and so on. We end up living in a world that's made up almost entirely of concepts and emotions.

Mind and Emotions

When we talk about "emotions," we generally understand that we're talking about heightened states of feeling. We often regard our emotions as a mixed blessing; they can be challenging states, but they're also precious to us. We see them as ennobling, as well as devastating. Because of their power, emotions can carry us beyond ordinary self-interest to inspire acts of courage and self-sacrifice, or feed our desires to the extent that we're driven to betray those we love and should protect. In the arts, they would be more akin to poetry and music than to documentaries, for example. However, the English word *emotion* doesn't convey quite the same meaning as "emotion" in the Buddhist sense. The difference is that, in the Buddhist context, the word *emotion* always refers to a state of mind that is agitated, disturbed, afflicted, under the sway of ignorance, and generally confused. The quality of agitation or disturbance means that emotional mind is a mental state that lacks clarity; due to that, it's also a state that causes us to act thoughtlessly and often unwisely. Accordingly, emotions are regarded as states of mind that obscure our awareness and therefore interfere with our capacity to see the true nature of mind. On the other hand, feelings that enhance the experience of openness and clarity, such as love, compassion, and joy, are not regarded as "emotions" in this sense; instead, they're seen as positive mental factors that are aspects of wisdom or qualities of awakened mind. However, any strong feeling—even if we label it "love"—that's governed by possessiveness, mundane attachment, self-gratification, or control issues is an ordinary emotion.

Hardened Values

Because truly direct experiences of the world are not often present in our ordinary life, we find ourselves living either in concepts or in an emotional world of past or future. And when our concepts become solidified, when they become so deeply ingrained in the fabric of our mind that they seem to be part of our being, that's when they become what we call "values." All cultures have their values and principles, but if we accept them blindly, without reference to their personal and cultural subjectivity, then they can become a source of confusion, of judgments about the legitimacy of other ideas or even the value of a human life. Yet values are no different from our other concepts in that they come from this day-to-day mind; they are produced in the same way. We go so quickly from perception to concept to emotion, and from there, it's just one more step to value judgments, concepts so solidified that they've grown impervious to doubt and questioning.

Society in general seems to be especially focused on the idea of values—democratic values, religious values, family values—as a force for good and a protection against chaos and evil. Sometimes we judge what is "good and safe" and what is "bad and dangerous" by just one thing, like color. Take black and white. Is white the color of purity and innocence or of death? In Asia, white symbolizes death and is worn at funerals, but in the West, doctors and brides wear white because it's peaceful, safe, and comforting. In the West, we wear black to funerals; it's associated with what we fear—death. Yet if we want to appear fearless, powerful, rebellious, or mysterious, we wear black—just look at the streets of New York City.

It's good to ask ourselves how often our labels truly represent our reality and how often they misrepresent it. When I'm on an airplane these days, I look around to see who is on the plane with me. Sometimes

I'll think, "Wow, that guy over there looks dangerous. Is he going to blow up my plane today?" But when I see that the airplane is full of white people, I feel very comfortable, very safe. I feel that I'm with "good people," because there aren't many scary-looking passengers like me on board. But I know the guy next to me is probably feeling uncomfortable about me and thinking, "Wow, look at that evil person. Is he going to blow up my plane?"

We all have our values. More and more, everything seems to be about good and evil, right and wrong. These concepts are so solidified now that they're on the point of becoming a law. I wouldn't be surprised if a "good and evil" bill were put before Congress. And not only do we have mundane labels to define good and evil, right and wrong, for us; on top of that, we have religious labels to help us further, or to make it even worse. All religions seem to be trying to scare us into doing the right thing—or else.

Stuck in the Conceptual World

When we don't pay attention, the conceptual world takes over our whole being. That's a pretty sad thing. We can't even enjoy a beautiful sunny day, watching leaves blowing in the wind. We have to label it all so that we live in a concept of sun, a concept of wind, and a concept of moving leaves. If we could leave it there, it wouldn't be too bad, but that never happens. Then it's "Oh yeah, it's good to be here. It's beautiful, but it would be better if the sun were shining from another angle." When we're walking, we're not really walking; a concept is walking. When we're eating, we're not really eating; a concept is eating. When we're drinking, we're not really drinking; a concept is drinking. At some point, our whole world dissolves into concepts.

As the external world is reduced to a conceptual world, we not only lose a wholesome part of our being, we lose all the beautiful things in the natural world: forests, flowers, birds, lakes. Nothing can bring us any genuine experience. Then our emotions come into play, supercharging our thoughts with their energy; we find there are "good" things that bring "good" emotions, and there are "bad" things that bring "bad" emotions. When we live our life like this every day, it becomes very tiresome;

we begin to feel a sense of exhaustion and heaviness. We may think that our exhaustion comes from our job or our family, but in many cases, it's not the job or family itself—it's our mind. What's exhausting us is how we relate to our life conceptually and emotionally. We risk becoming so stuck in the realm of concepts that nothing we do feels fresh, inspired, or natural.

These three—perceptual mind, conceptual mind, and emotional mind—are aspects of relative mind, our mundane consciousness, which we usually experience as a continuous stream. But in reality, perceptions, thoughts, and emotions last only for an instant. They're impermanent. They come and go so quickly that we're unaware of the discontinuity within this stream, of the space between each mental event. It's like watching a thirty-five-millimeter film. We know it's made up of many single frames, but due to the speed at which it moves, we never notice the end of one frame and the beginning of the next. We never see the imageless space between the frames, just as we never see the space of awareness between one thought and another.

We end up living in a fabricated world made up of these three aspects of relative mind. Layer by layer, we have constructed a solid reality that has become a burden, locked us into a small space, a corner of our being, and locked out much of who we really are. Usually, we think of a prison as something made of walls and prisoners as people locked inside, removed from the world for their crimes. Such inmates have basic routines that get them through the day, but the possibilities for a full experience and enjoyment of life are severely limited.

We are confined in a similar way, locked inside the prison walls of our conceptual world. The Buddha taught that what lies at the bottom of all this is ignorance: the state of not knowing who we truly are, of not recognizing our natural state of freedom and our potential for happiness, fulfillment, and enjoyment of life.

OUR NATURAL STATE OF FREEDOM

This ignorance is a kind of blindness that leads us to believe that the movie we're watching is real. As I mentioned earlier, when we believe that this busy mind—this stream of emotions and concepts—is who we truly are, it's like being asleep and dreaming without knowing we're dreaming. When we don't know we're asleep and in a dream state, we have no control over our dream life. The Buddha taught that the key to waking up and unlocking the door of our prison is self-knowledge, which extinguishes ignorance like a light being turned on in a room that has been dark for a very long time. The light immediately illuminates the whole room, regardless of how long it has been dark, and we can see what we haven't seen before—our true nature, our natural state of freedom.

Freedom can happen swiftly. One moment, we're bound by something, the sum total of our life—our concepts about who we are, our position in the world, the force and weight of our relationships to people and places; we're caught in the fabric of all that. Then, at another moment, it's gone. There is nothing obstructing us. We're free to walk out the door. In fact, our prison dissolves around us, and there's nothing to escape from. What has changed is our mind. The self that was caught, trapped, is freed the minute that the mind changes and perceives space instead of a prison. If there is no prison, then there can be no prisoner. In fact, there never was a prison except in our mind, in the concepts that became the brick and mortar of our confinement.

This is not to say that there are no real prisons—no jails or jailers, no forces in the world that can confine, inhibit, or restrict us. I'm not saying that it's all just a thought that can be swept away. We should not ignore any aspect of our reality. But even those prisons and negative forces arose from the thoughts of others; they're all products of someone's mind, someone's confusion. Even though we can't do much about that right away, we do have the power to work with our own mind now, and eventually we'll develop the wisdom to work with the minds of others.

UNCHANGING MIND

When the Buddha taught about this impermanent and composite (or "put together") nature of the relative mind, he did so in order to introduce his disciples to the ultimate nature of mind: pure, unfabricated, unchanging awareness. Here Buddhism departs radically from theological concepts like original sin that view humankind as spiritually tainted by some hereditary violation of divine law. The Buddhist view asserts that the nature of all beings is primordially pure and replete with positive qualities. Once we wake up enough to see through our confusion, we see that even our problematic thoughts and emotions are, at heart, part of this pure awareness.

Seeing this naturally brings us a sense of relaxation, joy, and humor. We don't need to take anything too seriously, because everything we experience on the relative level is illusory. From the point of view of the ultimate, it's like a lucid dream, the vivid play of mind itself. When we're awake in a dream, we don't take anything that happens in the dream too seriously. It's like going on the big rides at Disney World. One ride will take us up in the night sky with stars all around and the lights of a city below. It's so beautiful and we enjoy it, but we don't take it to be real. And when we ride through the haunted house, the ghosts, skeletons, and monsters might surprise us for an instant or two, but they're also funny, because we know they aren't real.

In the same way, when we discover the true nature of our mind, we're relieved from a fundamental anxiety, a basic sense of fear and worry about the appearances and experiences of life. The true nature of mind says, "Why stress out? Just relax and enjoy yourself." That's our choice, unless we have an exceptionally strong tendency to fight all the time; then even Disney World becomes a horrible place. That's also our choice. Our modern world is full of options these days, so wherever we are, we can do it either way.

Many people have asked what this kind of awareness is like. Is the experience of this "true nature" like becoming a vegetable, being in a coma, or having Alzheimer's? No. In fact, it's nothing like that. Our relative mind becomes better functioning. When we take a break from our habitual labeling, our world becomes clear. We're free to see clearly; think clearly; and feel the living, wakeful quality of our emotions. The openness, spaciousness, and freshness of the experience make it a beautiful place to be. Imagine standing on a scenic mountain peak and looking at the world in all directions without any obstructions. That is what's called the experience of the nature of mind.

FREEING OURSELVES FROM IGNORANCE

If knowledge is the key to our freedom, then how do we move from a state of unknowing to knowing? The logic of the Buddhist path is very simple. We begin from a state that is confused and dominated by ignorance; by cultivating knowledge and insight through study, contemplation, and meditation, we free ourselves from ignorance and arrive at a state of wisdom. Therefore, the essence of this path is the cultivation of our intelligence and the development of our insight. As we work with our intelligence, it becomes sharper and more penetrating; finally, it becomes so sharp that it cuts through the very concepts and ignorance that keep us bound to suffering. What we're doing is training our mind to free itself; we're exercising, working out, pumping up our rebel buddha.

Intelligence is not simply quantitative, a matter of how much we know. It is active; it functions. It's the arms and legs of the wisdom to which it's attached. It's what gets us moving and gets us to our goal. When we begin to break through those conceptual barriers, we not only change ourselves, but we begin to change the world around us. It's not always easy. It requires great conviction because we're challenging what is closest to us—our definition of self, both our personal self and the self of others. Whether it's a suffering self or a tyrannical self, it's what we know and have always cherished. But when you see the reality of your true self, you see it nakedly—stripped of all concepts. It's one thing to say, "The emperor has no clothes," and another thing to declare that and be the emperor yourself.

THE MYTH OF THE SELF

Imagine that you look down at your hand one day and see that it's clenched in a fist. You sense that you're holding on to something so vital that you can't let it go. Your fist is clenched so tightly that your hand hurts. The ache in your hand travels up your arm, and tension spreads throughout your body. This goes on for years. You take aspirin now and then, have a drink, watch TV, or take up skydiving. Life goes on, and then one day you forget about it, and your hand opens: there is nothing inside. Imagine your surprise.

The Buddha taught that the root cause of our suffering—ignorance— is what gives rise to this tendency to "cling." The question you should ask yourself is, "What am I clinging to?" We should look deeply at this process to see if anything is there. According to the Buddha, what we're clinging to is a myth. It's just a thought that says "I," repeated so often that it creates an illusory self, like a hologram that we take to be solid and real. With every thought, every emotion, this "self" appears as thinker and experiencer, yet it's really just a fabrication of mind. It's an ancient habit, so ingrained in us that this very clinging becomes part of our identity as well. If we weren't clinging to this thought of "me," we might feel that something familiar was missing—like a close friend or a chronic pain that suddenly disappears.

Just like gripping an imaginary object, our self-clinging doesn't accomplish much for us. It only gives us a headache and ulcers, and we quickly develop many other kinds of suffering on top of that. This "I" becomes very proactive in protecting its own interests, because it immediately perceives "other." The instant we have the thought of "I" and "other," the whole drama of "us" and "them" develops. It all happens in the blink of an eye: we cling to the "I" side and decide whether the "other" is for us, against us, or merely inconsequential. Finally, we set our agenda: toward one object, we feel desire and want to attract it; toward another, we feel fear and hostility and want to repel it; and toward another, we feel indifference and simply ignore it. Thus, the birth of our neurotic emotions and judgments is the result of our clinging to "I," "me," and "mine." Nor are we exempt from our own judgments. We admire some of our qualities and build ourselves up, disdain others and tear ourselves down, and ignore much of the pain we're really feeling because of this inner struggle to be happy with who we are.

Why do we persist in this when we would feel so much better and more relaxed if we just let go? The true nature of our mind is always present, but because we don't see it, we grasp what we do see and try to make it into something it's not. Such complications seem to be the only way the ego can survive—by creating a maze or a hall of mirrors. Our neurotic mind becomes so full of twists and turns that it's difficult to keep track of what it's doing. We expend all of this effort just to convince ourselves that we have found something solid within the insubstantial nature of our mind: a single, permanent identity—something we can call "me." Yet in doing so, we're working against the way things truly are. We're trying to freeze our experience, to create something solid, tangible, and stable out of something that doesn't have that character. It's like asking space to be earth or water to be fire. We think that to give up this thought of "I" would be crazy; we think our life depends on it. But actually, our freedom depends on letting it go.

buddha on the road

WHEN THE FIRST wave of Buddhist teachers began arriving in the United States in the late 1950s and the 1960s, the country was less than two hundred years old. Compared to the ancient civilizations of the East, it was like a child still asking, "Who am I? What do I want to be when I grow up?" Even today, we hear questions like, "Who are the real Americans? What are genuine American values?" The first Buddhist teachers to arrive in this "new world" brought with them not only the teachings of the Buddha, or *dharma*, but also their old-world cultures. Some lived here, adopted this culture, and learned its language. Others visited without embracing American culture or language. These teachers made a tremendous effort to establish the Buddha's teachings in the West. Although there were inevitably some cultural conflicts and misunderstandings, they showed great trust in their Western students, who trusted and opened their hearts to these teachers in return.

Nevertheless, every presentation of the Buddhist teachings was somewhat cultural, from the setup of the shrines to the code of ethics in the shrine room. This was necessary at the time, to some degree. The hippies of the sixties were going through a revolution of mind. They wanted nothing less than to change the culture of the West and free their society from its own rigid social structures and values. Having a new and exotic spirituality from far beyond the land of their birth was very appealing. It even became a key to the transformation of the time.

Why should we look back twenty-six hundred years, or even fifty, when we're here now, worrying about our own lives? Why write about this at all? There's a need to reflect on the history of dharma coming to the West and ask some questions: "Why are we developing a lineage of American Buddhism and a Buddhism for the West and modern cultures altogether? Who is this dharma for?" It is simply to help those of us living here and now to discover the same truth that the Buddha discovered centuries ago. That truth doesn't change. It doesn't go in and out of fashion over time. However, it does need to be accessible, and in my view, what it will take for us to "get it" is another revolution of mind.

A Revolution Felt around the World

The decade of the sixties stands out in my mind as an example of a cultural and spiritual revolution because it occurred in my lifetime. Although I was born halfway around the world at the beginning of this movement, it affected me personally. You could say it was a revolution that was felt around the world. It spread out from the United States to Europe and parts of Asia. It was certainly felt in Buddhist Asia, as Western hippies, scholars, poets, and musicians—as well as dopers—started showing up in the ashrams, monasteries, and zendos of the old world. Some came chanting "Om" and seeking knowledge, revelation really, about the nature of the mind and the universe. It was not long before I heard my first rock'n'roll songs—the Rolling Stones, Beatles, Bob Dylan, and Elton John—on what we called a *gramophone* in my small monastery village in the Indian foothills of Sikkim. My first young foreign friends were from America, and gradually I made friends from other places around the world: Europe, England, and Southeast Asia.

For me, this new generation—the hippie flower children—became the face of the world's changing times and future direction. This young generation formed a powerful counterculture that rejected establishment values; questioned authority; and engaged in freethinking, experimental lifestyles, and something new called "consciousness raising." They left their mainstream cultures and protested the war; marched for civil rights, women's rights, gay rights, and the endangered environment; and listened to their own rebel music like "Get It While You Can," "All You Need Is Love," and "Sympathy for the Devil."

Among the young, there was a sense of excitement and hope that the world was changing. They looked outward and saw a materialistic and moralistic society; they looked within and saw new dimensions of experience, hints of a transcendent reality, a new world, the possibility that heaven on earth was here right now, if they could only see it. It was just a glimpse, but it made a difference. As short-lived as it was, the impact of that fresh inspiration and rebel spirit is still being felt.

The desire for freedom—not just external freedom, but the state of being free—is transformative. Every step we take toward freedom helps to create a trail that others may follow, whether it's social, political, or spiritual. These three realms are not absolutely separate in any case. Nor are they, as I've said before, the unique possession of any nation or culture.

Although the sixties revolution faded, some aspects of its vision proved enduring. Certain social and civil liberties were achieved, or at least the doors for their achievement were opened. In my view, the most profound effect was spiritual—the dawning of a spiritual sensitivity and sense of quest for truth reminiscent of the days of Siddhartha, when the young gathered in the forests to debate, learn, and wholeheartedly work out their own road to freedom.

THE WORLD HAS CHANGED

Now, we're at the beginning of the twenty-first century. Look around at your neighbors: all the old Volkswagen-driving hippies have long since cut their hair and shaved their beards. They now look like the establishment they once rebelled against. The peace and love generation gave way to the ambitious generation—the Saab-driving yuppies. Then came the worried generation, Gen Xers, who inherited more problems than wealth. Now their kids—Gen Y and beyond—are waiting in the wings, playing video games until it's their turn to make their mark. The world has changed and keeps changing. No more "free love" and all those things that went on without much concern during the hippie revolution. They may have been appropriate for those days, but the times and the culture have changed. People have changed—the needs and psychology of men, women, and families are different. Prices are higher; opportunities for employment are different. Some jobs have disappeared, while new ones are hopefully taking their place.

We could still grow long hair and beards and take LSD. We could still drive Volkswagens covered with graffiti. But now everyone would laugh at us and say, "Look! He's pretending to be a hippie!" You'll never become a genuine hippie by pretending. Being a hippie was not just a matter of adopting a certain look or the marks of a certain lifestyle. There was a purpose for everything they did in that cultural and historical context. However, if you were to adopt those same forms today—the hair, drugs, free love, and a VW van—it wouldn't make sense. What you were doing would be out of context. It would be like a cheap imitation— something that no longer has any heart or philosophy behind it. You'd be better off with a shaved head, smoking pot at home. I think many people do this anyway, so at least it would be truer to the times.

The world we live in today is a different place. If the Buddha's teaching is to remain relevant, we can't hold on to our old hippie-era presentation of it. We can't drag it into the twenty-first century unchanged. When Buddhism arrived in America, it was all new. There was no similar meditative tradition here that could welcome and absorb the Buddhist teachings. To enter the tradition and learn its secrets, students took the path of immersion as the most genuine and productive route. You were a Zen student, a Tibetan Buddhist, or a Vipassana student who learned the teachings through the forms and protocols of those traditions. The candles and incense, the offering bowls and Buddha statues, the ringing of gongs and chanting in foreign tongues, the meditation cushions and elegant wall hangings combined to create an effect that was both beautiful and contemplative. It was also a bit foreign, even otherworldly. What was purely cultural, and what constituted the actual teaching? Who could tell in the beginning?

THE MASK OF CULTURE

Now we must look at what will help us benefit from this path today. Just as it makes no sense to hang on to the countercultural forms of the sixties, it is senseless to hang on to the forms of a traditional, Asian Buddhist culture and pretend we can fully inhabit that experience in a meaningful way. Since we're only in the beginning stages of developing a genuinely Western tradition of Buddhism, naturally we still need to rely on the cultures that are already old hands at this. They have much to teach us, but we must not be naïve about it. We shouldn't mistake their cultures for the wisdom itself. We shouldn't regard any particular form as sacrosanct.

The ancient Buddhist traditions of the East gave rise to elegant and powerful cultural forms. These forms are, in many cases, exquisitely expressive of the wisdom they contain. In style and substance, they're so integrated with that wisdom, so in tune with it, that the forms themselves can transmit an experience of wisdom to those who speak its language. But this didn't happen overnight. It took time and the insight of countless generations to discover and then refine these forms, some of them quite elaborate, which can open a door for us. Once we walk through that door, however, we're met with a paradox: the forms disappear. On the other side, there are no statues of buddhas, no incense bowls, no sound of gongs or chanting, no tatami mats or brocades, no meditation cushions, and no meditators. Why? These forms and activities are simply the means to enter the open dimension of our own mind. The wisdom they point to has no tangible form of its own. You can't hold wisdom in your hands, admire its brilliant colors, and put it on a shelf with your other prized possessions. You can't be sure of its color or shape or even where it really is. The mind that knows—our wakeful awareness—is formless.

Culture, on the other hand, is the tangible expression of our human experience. Our culture includes the art we make, the clothes we wear, and the language we speak. It includes the institutions we create, the religions we practice, the rituals we perform, and the concepts and beliefs through which we view and interpret our world. Culture is the fabric that holds together and identifies a society. It is passed from one generation to another, yet it is always in flux, changing as it interacts with new ideas and other cultures.

We can look at culture as a manifestation of our shared human experience. However, it's also an aspect of our individual experience, a "culture of the mind." Society's culture may provide us with a broad sense of our identity, but we each develop an individual sense of identity within our culture. We may be "Northerners" or "Southerners" but we're not stereotypes. We're not just like everyone else, even in our community or family. We may conform on some levels, but we always manage to express our uniqueness within that sameness. We have our own personality, our own style. When we look in the mirror, we see a distinctive physical reflection. But we also see somebody who dresses a certain way; has a distinct lingo; likes certain music, food, and movies and dislikes others. This reflection also has opinions, beliefs, and values as well as habits of thinking, feeling, and behavior that make us unique.

Altogether these attributes are what we take to be "me" or "my personality." The word *personality* comes from the Latin word *persona,* meaning "a mask." That mask is what other people see. In a sense, we speak from behind this face. Since we possess this personality, it seems natural to express it. Everything we create—from our mask to our family to businesses to governments to art—contributes, in turn, to the creation of the culture we live in. So it's not hard to see how our world and its institutions and values arise from the mind—my mind and your mind, our mind and their mind, one mind after the other and all of them together. Who we are is shaped by our culture, and who we are is what changes it as well. Each person is a part of the social fabric, influenced by it and exerting an influence on it in turn. Because of this interdependence, we can't really say that we as individuals or that our culture as a whole exist separately or independently. We can say that wherever there is mind, there is culture, and wherever there is culture, there is mind.

MEETING THE BUDDHA

The Buddha said long ago that when anyone in the future met with his teachings, it would be the same as meeting him in person. Therefore we can "meet the Buddha" today in the form of teachers, teachings, or our own practice. Saying we want to meet the Buddha is like saying we want to meet the awakened state of our own mind. We don't have to change who we are in order to meet the Buddha in this way. The purpose of our meeting is not to become a student of another culture or to discover someone else's wisdom. We're not practicing Indian culture to become Indian, or practicing Japanese or Tibetan culture to become Japanese or Tibetan. Our purpose is to discover who we truly are, to connect with our own wisdom.

The best way to meet the Buddha is to invite him into our home. When we're studying or practicing his teachings, the Buddha is there. We don't have to redecorate our home to look like a monastery or like a house in an Indian village in order to look at our mind. And we don't need a traditional white scarf and Indian tea to welcome a visit from a present-day Tibetan teacher. When we first meet, we might greet him with a traditional Asian form of respect, such as bowing, but at later meetings, we might offer a handshake. We can serve our guest the traditional tea, but we can also offer a different drink—a Coke or a Starbucks latte. We can discuss meditation, share meals, or watch movies together. Over time, an exchange takes place, and we develop a mutual respect and friendship. We discover that, while there is a great deal we can learn from this accomplished teacher, we have something to offer as well. We have a wealth of experience and knowledge accumulated from our life to share. We're not merely recipients in this relationship between cultures; we're contributors to a dialogue that enriches both worlds.

the way to go

WHAT IS THE Buddhist spiritual journey like for someone who decides to travel this road? What is the essence of the experience? What do you do, what do you confront, and how does that change you?

The Buddhist path has its own learning curve, as does life itself. When you're a kid, your parents take care of you; but when you strike out on your own, you enter a whole new world. The challenges you face all at once—learning a new job and managing relationships, time, money, and your own household—may seem overwhelming at first. You have no idea whether or not you can do it; you have no idea if it will all get easier tomorrow or next year. You don't know because you've never been through this before; you have no frame of reference for something of this magnitude. So in the beginning, the support and encouragement of parents, mentors, and friends help you, yet you know you must do this on your own. There is no way out of it.

In the same way, on your spiritual journey, you start out not knowing much. But as you continue, you become more learned, competent, and confident, which sparks more energy and interest in your subject. Here the subject in general is mind, and in particular, it's your own mind. There is an aspect of traditional study, working with teachers and so on, but the most crucial aspect of the path is the "hands-on" part, where you work directly with your own mind and experience.

When you start to study your mind, you begin to see how mind works. You discover the principle of cause and effect; you see that certain actions produce suffering and others produce happiness. Once you make that discovery, you understand that by working with suffering's causes, you can overcome suffering itself. You also begin to see, in the contents of mind, a clearer picture of your own psychological profile. That is, you begin to see the patterns of thought and feeling that repeat over and over. You see how predictable you are in your relationships and interactions with the world. You come to see, too, how ephemeral the contents of mind are. At a certain point, you begin to glimpse the total space of mind, the brilliant awareness that is the source of your fleeting thoughts and emotions. This is your first look at mind's true nature; it's a milestone on your path and an experience of personal freedom.

Your initial studies are important because they show you the terrain of your journey, like a good map. A map will show you where there are highways, byways, crossroads, and dead ends. It will show you where there are mountains and valleys, cities and empty spaces. You can see where you are and where you're going. In this way, you can begin to prepare yourself for each part of your trip. What follows in this book is a description of the journey from an experiential perspective. It is an orientation to the Buddha's map.

We know that our final destination is freedom and that the way to understand both freedom and our lack of it lies in working with our mind. In the beginning, there are certain lessons to be learned and realities to be faced. These are simply moments of recognition of the human condition, yet if we take them to heart, they're transformative. The most fundamental of these moments are the recognition of our aloneness and our suffering and the realization that the power to transform our life is always in our hands. Thus, the path begins with reflection and developing our motivation; it then proceeds with learning the specific methods for working with our own mind.

ME FIRST: DISCOVERING PERSONAL FREEDOM

The most critical part of the spiritual journey is the beginning. How do we begin? The Buddha taught that first we need to focus on ourselves, on gaining what we call "individual freedom." This means that your personal freedom is at stake, not the freedom of anyone else, including your best friend, lover, or family. It's also not about the freedom of your community, nation, or the whole world. This is about you, as an individual. You begin with who and how you are right now; it's your neurotic self, the illusion of ego, that's starting off on the road to freedom. What other self is there to wake up and free from suffering?

The impulse toward personal freedom and happiness is natural to everyone. It's a basic desire of the human heart. "Do you want to be free from suffering? Do you want to be happy?" Ask anyone those questions, and without exception, everybody's answer would be the same: "Yes, that's what I'm looking for. That's why I've taken this nine-to-five job. That's why I'm going to night school. That's why I'm taking the red-eye special and then walking straight into a conference room. That's why I'm quitting this job. That's why I'm getting married. That's why I'm getting divorced."

Everything we do is, on some level, an expression of this desire for freedom and happiness. Often, however, the methods we use to become freer and happier don't accomplish what we hope. I remember the first days of the Internet and high-speed computers. I heard many comments from my Western friends like, "Oh, it's going to be a really great tool. We'll have more free time, because computers will make our work much easier and more efficient." I'm sure they thought they would have more time to spend with their families and go on vacations to Mexico or the Caribbean Islands. But with all these helpful gadgets and tools, we find ourselves even busier than before. Your e-mail chases after you when you're having a nice dinner with your friends. Your BlackBerry beeps and you can't resist looking at your next message, even though your friend is trying to say something to you. So if you can't even be free at dinner, then forget about the rest of those freedoms you imagined that computers would deliver.

It's the same with all our material possessions, if our desire to have them is based on the hope that they'll free us in any way from the suffering of our basic insecurity, worry, identity crisis, or just plain boredom. Even though we say we know better, we still believe that the new house, new car, new laptop, or new flat-screen hi-def TV is going to give us a boost, change our life somehow. Then we have the bank chasing after us for the mortgage, the car insurance to keep up, and the same old programs on the new TV. I'm not sure how much happiness we actually get from these things; they seem to include a measure of suffering, which we may have signed on for when we checked the "I accept these terms and conditions" box.

What's going on here is not that we have the wrong desire, but that we're going about getting what we want in the wrong way. We're mistaken about the "how" part in how to be happy and free. Sometimes we even turn the freedom we do have into a cause of suffering. If you have friends or family coming over all the time, then you feel that you're losing your privacy. You have no freedom, and you complain about it: "Give me some space! I need space, please." You could just take your laptop and go to a café where there's free Wi-Fi; however, what you feel like doing is kicking everybody out. But on the other hand, if nobody shows up, what do you do? Complain again: "Nobody comes to see me. I'm so lonely." So we're stuck in this dilemma. We go back and forth, wanting one thing, then another, creating more and more inner conflict for ourselves because we haven't found a way to simply be happy. No matter how much freedom we have, there's still a sense of struggle. We always seem to be fighting for more freedom or a different kind of freedom, and therefore the suffering is endless.

Your Own Experience Is What Counts

When the Buddha taught the importance of individual freedom, he was giving us a very simple but profound instruction: before doing anything else, you must first connect with all your heart to your desire to be free. Then you can begin to learn the most effective methods for fulfilling your desire. This means that your individual path must be connected to your own unique experience of life. Each of us needs to look at our own experience of suffering to see how it is distinct; we don't suffer in the exact same way as anybody else. What causes me to suffer may not cause you to suffer. What is extremely hard for you may be easy or even fun for me. What you enjoy doing may be frightening or boring for me. And so it goes. When you reach the point of being determined to be freed from your suffering, you have the attitude that starts you off on the path of individual freedom: "I will deliver myself from harm; I will protect and save myself from heartache and misery." This is where you start.

You shouldn't be afraid of this individualistic focus. You might think that to concentrate on yourself to the exclusion of others would lead to greater problems of egotism, pride, and other nonspiritual qualities. Ordinarily, that might be the case. But here we combine that focus with training our mind in a way that develops self-discipline and leads to genuine spiritual knowledge. There's nothing wrong with being individualistic; it becomes problematic only when it's misdirected. If you can point this sense of individualism in the right direction, then it becomes very positive. What will help you find your direction is to stop what you're doing and just look at your true condition in life. When you do that, you either freak out or get your bearings pretty quickly. And what is that true condition? There are many types of suffering, but there's one that's worth contemplating above all others: nothing lasts. Life is short, the clock never stops ticking, and the time of your death will be a surprise.

You Are Alone

Cultivating our individualism makes sense, because we're clearly alone in the world. We must face that and learn to be independent. From the time we emerged from our mother's womb and the umbilical cord was cut, we have been alone. The cutting of the cord is so symbolic. From that moment forward, we have to start learning to be independent, beginning with breathing on our own.

Of course, there are many people who help us along the way—parents, nannies, family, and friends. But still, as you grow up, you're growing up alone. When they send you off to school, you go alone, even though there are hundreds of other kids there. You have to get through each day yourself. You're alone when you're studying and alone when you take your exams. Even your best friends can't help you pass them. When you graduate, you're alone, wearing that square cap. When you need to get a job, you've got to do it yourself, and when you find one, no one but you is responsible for the work you do. Regardless of how many other people you have in your life, ultimately you have to help yourself become the person you want to be.

We may not be conscious of it, but the reality of our aloneness is with us all the time, and we feel it in different ways. We might experience it as a sense of dissatisfaction or restlessness, or we may feel undercurrents of anxiety or depression. Wherever we are or whatever we're doing in a given moment, it never seems to be quite enough; something's always missing. When you're sitting inside your house and looking out the window, you want to go outside; after you're outside for five minutes, you feel like it's better inside. You wander aimlessly from your desk to the kitchen, and then ask yourself why you're there—you're not hungry or thirsty. You turn on the TV but keep changing the channels. If you don't have a partner, you dream of the happiness you'd have with your ideal mate. But when that person is sleeping right next to you, you're still not entirely at peace. There is rarely a sense of simple contentment. It's a never-ending process, the search for whatever we think "it" is that will fill the empty space that exists within all our experiences.

Whatever our desires may be, getting the object of our desire is not the same thing as contentment, which comes from within. In the end, we'll never find complete contentment, a perfect sense of peace, if our mind isn't content and at peace. You could be successful in your career and making your target salary. You could have money in the bank, a spouse, five kids, a house, and a nice car with a Mini Uzi in the glove compartment. You could have the American dream in your pocket and still feel that you need something else. In that case, it's your mind that's poor—not your life or bank account. Contentment doesn't mean we're lazy, just sitting around, satisfied with whatever. It means that we experience a sense of fulfillment and joy. If we're content, then we're rich even if we only have a few dollars in our wallet. But if we have no contentment, then we'll suffer even with a million dollars under our mattress.

From Problem to Possibility

When we're caught up in a confused, agonizing state of mind, the best way to free ourselves from it is to fully experience that pain. That's what will inspire in us the determination and commitment we need to go beyond our habitual patterns. It's only by relating to our fundamental pain in a direct and genuine way that we develop real enthusiasm for the path of individual freedom. Suffering is a problem for us only when we can't see any possibility of freeing ourselves from it. When we're willing to work with our pain, it becomes a productive experience. It is what causes us to want to be free. Otherwise, how would we even form the idea of freedom—freedom from what? Suffering makes our aspiration much more powerful by making it real. It acts like a catalyst; it boosts our resolve to work with our mind.

At the same time, it's important not to lose sight of where we're going with all this determination. We must keep our goal of liberation in mind, or else our efforts might become half-hearted, and if they are, they won't work. If we lose sight of the big picture, then our determination may come and go, depending on how good or bad we feel on any given day. When we're comfortable, our resolution doesn't feel so urgent. We can do something else for a while and work with our mind later, when we feel worse. Sometimes we think, "It's a nice day. Why can't I just take a break from it all?" That's fine—just don't end up stuck between two worlds, more miserable than ever. You see your freedom off in the distance and the view is nice, but it's like looking at a picture of a paradise you know you'll never visit in person.

When we meet suffering in person, in a moment of disappointment or anger or jealousy, we shouldn't say to it, "Go away, you're disturbing me and making me feel bad." Instead, we can look at it directly and say, "I've seen you before, and here you are again. I've avoided this moment, but now it's time to face you straight on and clear up a few things. I know you've been helping me, so thank you for that. But now I'd like to say good-bye. I'm walking toward the path of liberation."

Power of the Heart

It takes a strong sense of resolve to be certain in our heart that we don't want to face our suffering with the same old mind of confusion and ignorance. We don't want to perpetuate the same old habitual patterns that do nothing but make us feel lost and ensure that our suffering will reappear, perhaps in a more intense form. We can tell ourselves, "From today onward, I really want to be free, to liberate myself from this suffering and pain." Otherwise, if we're counting on a miracle or some form of heavenly intervention without making our own effort, it's like hiring a bad hitman. We keep waiting for him to do the job he was hired to do, but nothing happens. In the end, we realize that the person we hired to get rid of our problem isn't going to do it. We have to shoot our ignorance ourselves, point-blank.

The point is that, spiritually, we're responsible for ourselves. That's the basic principle of this nontheistic journey. You can't look up and say with confidence that someone's there, somewhere above you, who will save you, so long as you keep your part of the bargain—to show up at the scheduled times and places and pay your dues. There's no deal on the books to fall back on. You can't carry on with your godfather-like business dealings and think that, in the end, you'll be saved because you're part of the family. From the Buddhist point of view, you take this journey on your own, and the only person who can save you is you.

Sometimes, in order to really develop this sense of one-pointed determination, it's necessary to suffer a lot. If you have a slight headache, for instance, then you may be too lazy to do anything about it; but if you have a migraine headache, then you'll take whatever steps are necessary to free yourself from it. When we have a little suffering here and there, we can get distracted and ignore it, but when we have real suffering, then we start to pay attention and do something about it. For example, when people struggle with substance abuse or other addictions, they often have to "hit bottom" with their addiction before they finally feel truly motivated to commit to recovery.

When you find yourself in a situation where you feel you have no hope whatsoever, that's the exact point where you can begin to feel a sense of real liberation. When you're desperate, when you've lost everything and have no control over what's happening to you—that's when the teachings can make a real impact. They're not theoretical at that point. When you've hit bottom in your life and are suffering deeply, that's the time to be strong. Don't give up; instead, look at yourself and say, "Enough is enough. I won't get caught in this pattern again. Today is the day it ends." Right then and there you connect with the power of your rebel buddha heart and the mind of individual liberation, and you are on your road to freedom.

Renouncing the Causes of Suffering

When your own painful experiences inspire you to the extent that you become truly determined to break free of suffering, that is what the Buddha taught as the attitude of "renunciation." You see your suffering, you feel your aloneness, and you're saddened by the dissatisfaction that runs through your life. Now you feel ready to face this tenacious cycle of unhappiness, discover its true causes, and uproot them.

We might say—and truly believe—that we're already doing everything we can to avoid suffering. But if we look more closely, we might see that, while hating our pain, we seem to love many of the things that cause it. So there's a slight disconnect between our intentions and our behavior. It's like having revulsion for the hangover but finding drinking very appealing. The problem is, as much as we think we want to be free of our suffering, we keep repeating the patterns of behavior that perpetuate it. Not only are we habituated to these causes, like indulging in fits of anger or jealousy, but we even enjoy the excitement we feel when we give in to them.

It's obvious from this that we don't really know much about the mechanism of cause and effect in regard to our suffering. This is what the Buddha meant when he said, "Everyone wants to be happy, but we constantly destroy our own happiness as if it were our enemy." So a good part of our path in the beginning is investigating cause and effect and seeing how they operate in our life. Doing this changes how we see things. Something that we were once attracted to and indulged in mindlessly—like gossiping about our coworkers—suddenly looks like terrible behavior once we understand its effects. Our gossiping actually hurts others and, indirectly, ourselves. It's not an innocent act. Once we connect the dots between cause and result, we develop an attitude of revulsion toward actions we once thought nothing of. We see that we're often miserable, not because the world is against us, but simply because we have acted on impulse, without thinking.

Dealing with Desire

Impulse is related to desire, which is a deeper and more sustained level of feeling. We can experience a sense of free-floating desire that has no particular object, but our desire tends to quickly form attachments to all the nice things we see, hear, smell, taste, and feel. Once desire has an object, we want to possess that object. That may mean we just want to hold it in our mind and appreciate it for a while, like a beautiful mountain view. Or it may mean we go a little crazy and start obsessing over something, like a romantic trip to the south of France. Much of what we do and say is based simply on desire. We want something and reach out to grab it with no thought of the consequences, no gap in the process that might allow us to see if it's something we really want. It may be a new romance, a new car, or the satisfaction of revenge. It's a powerful feeling, a kind of hunger that drives away all thought except that of putting something, anything, into your mouth. The first taste is so sweet, and you're happy for a moment, but you don't know if what you're swallowing is rotten or poisonous or if it will make you sick.

Desire is both compelling and blind. It has the power to intoxicate, to make us enthusiastic at the same time that it diminishes our capacity for clear thinking. I'm sure you know the feeling. The point is that we need to understand how desire works with the mechanism of cause and effect. When the energy of desire combines with the force of our habitual patterns, we need to remember our other desire—for individual freedom—and invoke our rebel buddha mind; otherwise, we may end up lost in the wilderness or bankrupt in a foreign country.

Suffering, however, is not always caused by something we think of as negative. It can also be the result of something we like and want, like wealth, fame, power, or success. Any ordinary source of happiness, if we become overly attached to it, can become a cause of suffering. We only need to watch the news to see how many people end up suffering every day because of their attachment to wealth. Whether you're a stockbroker, a drug dealer, or a lottery winner, you don't really know if you'll be laughing or crying in the end. In some cases, your money or desire for it could land you in jail or cause your death.

We may have many kinds of ordinary happiness in our life, but it's rare for people to be truly content if their happiness depends mostly on material things or the opinions of others. Prince Siddhartha had great wealth and high social rank, yet he left them behind to look for an inner truth and peace of mind. The things that make up our ordinary happiness are all fine in and of themselves. In fact, they're good to have and enjoy; there's no need to reject them. But there's a danger if our attachment to them begins to blind us. Whether your desires are modest in scope, like getting that promotion and taking a cruise through the Greek Islands, or more ambitious, like taking over the company and hiring the *Queen Mary* 2 exclusively for you and a few friends, you need to watch your mind to see if you're truly getting happiness from these things or setting yourself up for further suffering.

We need to be wise, to have some sense of letting go of our desire and attachments even as we gather what we want. Otherwise, we're losing the whole point of our journey; we're accumulating the stuff of ordinary dreams and giving our freedom away. Eventually, we will have to face the truth of our own impermanence. It would be a great suffering to realize, just at the point of death, that all the work we'd done, all our efforts and accomplishments, were dedicated to things in which we could find no meaningful essence.

With that frame of mind, we next look at the causes we need to transform and the actual methods for doing so. The important point here is to understand that we gain our freedom, not by renouncing suffering itself, but by renouncing its causes. Once suffering appears, it's there and we must live through it. We can't go back in time and change the actions that caused it, just as we can't unplant the apple seed of the apple we're holding in our hand.

relating with confusion

WE'RE SOMETIMES too polite with our suffering and allow it to dominate our life. Instead, we can confront it and challenge its power to limit our happiness. When we do this, we're starting down a different road, headed in a new direction. Since our goal is to overcome confusion and fully wake up, we need to start by relating to the mind that's confused and working with that mind directly. So we need to go through some kind of training that will prepare us to work effectively with our mind. We need to develop certain skills, we need to learn how and when to apply these skills, and we need to understand the purpose of acquiring these skills in the first place.

Before we take on such training, however, it's helpful to see that the whole notion of "training" is not something extraordinary. It's a natural part of our experience of life. Training is part of growing up; it's how we develop as individuals and find our place in the world. It's also essential to see just what we're training. Or we could ask, "Why is all this training necessary?" We need to see that our mind is not just a busy mind, but also that there are areas of the mind that are in a state of darkness, or ignorance, similar to states of deep sleep. That darkness stops us from seeing clearly and doing things well. We need to shed light on these areas and make them more conscious—wake them up. Once they're awake, they can be trained. Finally, we practice mindfulness: watching the mind and bringing it back to the present moment again and again. That is perhaps the most essential component of any training. You can't be somewhere else mentally while your training is going on here.

Basic Training for Life

The idea of training and self-improvement is part of the fabric of Western culture. We're doing it all the time, in one way or another. Our training begins in our family life and continues in our school and work lives. We learn basic knowledge and skills, such as how to behave in a social setting. Once we've learned the fundamentals, they become the foundation for developing our own path in life. We may not think of this ordinary training we go through as a "path" in the same way that we think of our spiritual path, but we do recognize that any goal is preceded by the path that gets us there. You don't get to where you want to go just by pointing to a spot on a map. You don't become a doctor just by saying, "I want to be a doctor."

Basic training on the Buddhist path involves working with our whole being—body, speech, and mind. Nothing is left out. Our training in life covers the same territory. To train our body, we may go to the gym, take dance classes, learn yoga, and follow a healthy diet. If we want to run a marathon, dance in a ballet, or swim in the Olympics, then we can take our physical training much further.

Training in speech starts with the basic language skills, which then become our means for self-expression and communication. Everything we do is affected by our speech. It's how we form relationships, pass along information, and express our feelings. We need to know how to use it to say everything from "hello" to "good-bye"—and especially the simplest things, like "I love you" and "I'm sorry." There's a whole industry in the West devoted to improving communication skills. A standard question on job applications asks you to rate your communication skills. If you're in doubt about yours, you can ask your partner, who will probably be happy to tell you how you're doing in that area.

Training the mind involves both accumulating knowledge about our world and learning how to think clearly and critically. These are universal goals of our educational system. Once we're armed with knowledge and reason, we can see problems and solve them. We can recognize opportunities and take advantage of them. We have the means to understand our world and find a meaningful place in it.

What happens when we don't have this training? We're at a disadvantage in every aspect of our life. When we do have it, then body, speech, and mind become better functioning, more useful tools to help us achieve our goals. They work for and not against our happiness.

The Buddhist path is a similar "lifelong learning experience." The curriculum, however, is adjusted slightly to accomplish its objective: waking us up, rousing the mind that's asleep. So our education consists of learning how we do this. Primarily, it's a matter of training our mind, our natural wakeful intelligence, to disrupt the peace, so to speak, to make it difficult for us to remain comfortably asleep. Rebel buddha does this by shining the wakeful light of knowledge wherever the darkness of bewilderment, ignorance, or delusion hang out or hide within our mind. That's how we train to reach our goal of individual freedom. It takes work and understanding. You don't become buddha—awakened—just by snapping your fingers or clicking your heels.

Before we start training, we need to ask ourselves, "What exactly am I trying to accomplish or develop or improve? What is the purpose of these trainings?" Sometimes on a spiritual path, we don't bother to ask such questions. We're satisfied that we're generally on a course to being good. But we need to have a clearer and more concrete understanding of our objectives and how to reach them. In other words, we need to understand and take advantage of the principle of cause and effect on our spiritual path. We need to apply that logic.

THE MIND YOU ARE TRAINING

One objective of our training is to learn how to see the full picture of the mind in order to understand its problems and see what it needs. The Buddha taught that there are certain states of mind underlying our normal conscious activity that are closed in darkness, similar to a state of deep sleep. You can awaken a light sleeper with a gentle touch or soft sound, but someone in a deep sleep won't respond so easily. Here, we're working with deep mental states that are dull and unresponsive; they need oxygen and light to revive and stimulate them. When we get to know the mind more fully, we can see beyond the surface of the mind to this basic state of bewilderment and confusion.

Mind in Darkness

This mental state of darkness is a fundamental obstacle for us. In this state of unknowing bewilderment, there is no sense of openness, no sense of genuine knowledge or understanding. When this mind is dominant, we don't even know that we don't know. We aren't aware of being in the dark; furthermore, we have no interest in knowing. That's the main problem. We're not only deluded, but we're also not inquisitive. There is no sense of quest, no pursuit of knowledge. In this state of total darkness, we begin to blame others: "How was I supposed to know the speed limit is twenty-five miles per hour? There are no signs!;" or "I didn't know I was supposed to attend that meeting. Nobody told me!" That shows a lack of inquisitiveness. With a little more curiosity and less laziness, it wouldn't be that difficult to find out these things.

Another aspect of this general sense of bewilderment is a lack of self-awareness. We tend to be unconscious of ourselves and our actions. While we usually think we're quite conscious in everyday situations, many times we're clueless about what we're saying or doing—until it's too late. Then you think, "Oh s***, I shouldn't have said that to my partner. Now I'll be hearing about this for days." And you may be hearing about it for years. The point is that what you say and do can have a strong impact in the world beyond what you intend or imagine. That impact is not just about what you go through, but also what others—whomever you involve in your slipups—go through.

These two mental states—bewilderment and ignorance—are usually beyond our conscious perception. Nevertheless, they need to be transformed. To do that, you first need to recognize the experiences of having them. Then rebel buddha can begin to work with them and wake them up.

Mind in the Spotlight

Another aspect of mind that we need to look at more closely is our emotional mind. While the emotions are more easily seen, we don't know them as well as we think. We may see the immediate suffering they bring, but we usually don't see how we use our emotions as a basis for strengthening our self-clinging or self-importance, which is a deeper cause of suffering. We pull this off by identifying with our emotional states and then taking pride in being a certain kind of person: "I'm an angry person," "I'm a jealous person," or "I'm a lustful person." Whatever it is, it makes us special. We acquire a certain kind of prestige, at least in our own mind, because of our temperament. We're not just nobody, and we have our anger or our passion to prove it. In this way, our emotions become just another form of delusion.

The actual experience of emotions is a different story. They come and go naturally. When they come, they're full of color and energy, and when they go, there's nothing left. The key thing to remember is that when an emotion arises, it's just a simple thought in the beginning—nothing more. But then we take it further. We give our emotions our respect; we hold them in high esteem. They suddenly become very important—the superstars and big wheels of our thinking mind. In comparison, all other thoughts seem like boring chatter.

Sometimes we embrace an emotion so strongly that it triggers physical reactions. A sudden attack of anger can hit us like a shot of adrenaline and send our heart racing. A fit of jealousy can keep us awake all night long, spinning out storylines and justifications. But even on a day-to-day basis, we can carry emotional distress in our body in the form of various kinds of pain, from headaches to backaches to nausea. We might feel tired all the time but still can't sleep, or we feel so wired that we can't calm down. The longer and more tightly we cling to our emotions, the deeper and more pervasive their impact on us becomes. Yet even as we blame our emotions for the distress they bring, we pay tribute to them. Whether they take us closer to heaven or hell, we admire their unsurpassed power to move us.

It's a basic principle of the marketplace that all you need to do to sell something is to keep reinforcing the importance of your product. Eventually, everyone will want your gadget, whether they need it or not. In the same way, we're continually selling ourselves on the importance of our emotions, making ourselves into both seller and buyer, spin doctor and gullible public. Who profits from this arrangement? Who pays and for how long? The alternative is to realize that our emotions are part of our thought process in general, and the thought process is momentary. When you can say, "Oh, I'm having an angry thought or a jealous thought," that means you're aware of your experience and its fleeting nature. You're on your way to transforming it.

Hopeless Mind

Sometimes we give up on ourselves. Just as we fall into states of ignorance and delusion, we can also fall into states of mind that lack confidence. We start to look down on ourselves. We have no real self-esteem or self-respect. We don't trust our ability to travel the path and face its challenges. We may think we have a favorable impression of ourselves, but the trouble is that it doesn't go very deep. Beneath the surface of our optimism is a feeling of hopelessness. Just when we need courage and conviction to take another step in the direction of freedom, our confidence disappears.

We may also think that while the Buddha's teachings can help others, they can never help us. In this state of mind, we give up our resolve. If we fall into this mentality, we need to reconnect with our original inspiration and heart of determination. We need to tell ourselves, "Yes, I can do this. I can guide myself through this. I, too, have the potential to achieve my goal." Of course, we can still rely on the wisdom and compassion of the Buddha, the efficacy of the teachings, and the support of spiritual friends at the same time. There's no conflict in that; but ultimately we have to work out our own freedom. To reach our goal, we have to unlock the door and walk through it.

You have to trust that you're not a hopeless case, no matter how sleepy, wild, or crazy your mind seems to be. The way you develop this sense of trust on the Buddhist path is through the process of training your mind. That's how you realize for yourself that this road does, in fact, lead to freedom. Each of the trainings you go through in discipline, meditation, and higher knowledge helps you to see the relationship of cause and effect and accumulate the knowledge and skills you need to break free of your habitual patterns. By bringing greater mindfulness and awareness into your life, you develop a level of communication with your own mind that goes beyond anything in your past experience. You're getting closer to it, becoming more intimate and knowing in regard to its nature. The result is that you make a friend out of a stranger. When your relationship with your mind is based on trust instead of ignorance, fear, and hopelessness, your mind becomes calm, clear, and open. Then it becomes a support for whatever you wish to accomplish.

MINDFULNESS IS YOUR ALLY

For any kind of training to work, we have to be present in a conscious state. Our mind has to be there with our body. So one of the first things we learn is the practice of mindfulness. This is simply the practice of bringing ourselves fully into the present moment and continuing to bring ourselves back to it whenever we notice we've drifted away. So we have two things at play here: one is our awareness of being in the present, and the other is the mindfulness that sees us leaving the present and brings us back. If we're to stay focused in the present moment and conscious of our fresh experience, we need to be both mindful and aware.

The act of bringing your mind into the present is an act of self-discipline. The tendency of mind to move this way and that, from the present to the past, from the past to the future and back again, is brought to a halt. It's like when the bell rings at the beginning of class and the teacher calls the students to order. For a moment, all the chaos is dispelled, and there are a few precious seconds of quiet and simple, unified attention. Like small children, the mind has trouble remaining still for very long. It gets restless and starts to fidget. Any teacher will tell you that no learning can take place while kids are squirming in their seats. It's the same when we're training our mind. We need to remind ourselves to be present and pay attention.

All of our training relies on these two practices: mindfulness and awareness. Awareness is our consciousness of being in the present. Mindfulness means "to remember" or "not to forget" to watch the mind and see when it drifts away from the present. The moment we see that, we're back again. Without the activity of mindfulness, we get lost in the mind's continual flow of thoughts, and our awareness becomes like a child lost in a thick forest.

Of the two, mindfulness is usually emphasized more because it's responsible for maintaining the continuity of our awareness. Mindfulness means to remember again and again. It has a certain quality of repetitiveness. That's how we develop all of our habitual patterns, negative or positive—through repetition. So in this case, by cultivating a sense of mindful presence, we're establishing a positive tendency that has the power to transform any negative tendency.

When we're mindful, we notice the flow of things. There's a sense of continuity to our awareness, a complete experience of the present moment. Ordinarily, when we see something, we don't see it fully or clearly. Our seeing is interrupted by thoughts, concepts, and all kinds of distractions. That's why few people are really good witnesses. If you see a robbery and are questioned by the police, you say, "Yeah, I saw it, but, um, I don't really remember much about it." You can't say for sure who was holding the gun or how many shots were fired. Even our memories of vivid events are often vague. When we're present and alert and not distracted, however, there's nothing missing in our observations.

Together, mindfulness and awareness produce a quality of attention that's precise and clear. You're clear about your thoughts. You're clear about what you see, hear, and feel. When you're seeing something in a moment of nowness, you know precisely what's happening. There's a very fine precision beyond words.

We can look at it like this: our mind is like a house, and our mindfulness is like the tenant of that house. Because we don't want any intruders or unwelcome guests, we lock all the doors and windows of our house. Now no one can get in unless we let them in. No one can enter unannounced. That's the function of mindfulness—to be watchful of what's trying to enter our mind. If an angry thought tries to enter our mind, it can't come in until we open the door. Our purpose is not to shut everything out; it's to remain conscious of our environment and what's happening in it. Then we can deal with it appropriately. We can open the door to our angry thought, listen to it, and then ask it to leave.

We recognize it as a thought and don't mistake it for who we are. That's the point. It shifts the experience. Instead of thinking, "I'm really angry right now," we think, "Oh, look, an angry thought has entered my mind." It's easy to let go of a thought that's a guest in your mind; it's harder when you take on the identity of the guest. Who are you going to ask to leave?

No matter where we are or what we're doing, we can practice mindfulness. It is essential to all methods for working with body, speech, and mind. We can be out walking on the street, sitting in meditation, or reading a book. This practice is our greatest friend and ally on the spiritual path. It's the calling card of rebel buddha and the nemesis of ignorance.

the three trainings

THE VARIOUS METHODS of training the mind on the Buddhist path are the means we use to bring illumination, peace, and confidence to those states of mental darkness, agitation, and loss of heart that cause us suffering. This training is divided into three areas: discipline, meditation, and higher knowledge. Once you can relate to the idea of training yourself, once you know what it is you're training and agree to be present as much as possible during this process, then you can begin the actual three trainings. Each kind of training helps you wake up and achieve individual freedom.

DISCIPLINE: COOL, CALM, AND COLLECTED

When we talk about discipline, we're not talking about transforming a bad boy or girl into a good one. It doesn't mean beating your mind with a stick or whipping it into submission. And it's not a ploy to deprive your life of excitement or interest. Like the word *emotion, discipline* in the Buddhist sense has several meanings that are not apparent in common English usage. First, it carries the meaning of "cooling out." It's like being outside in the middle of a hot summer day, and just when you're feeling really beaten down by the heat, you find some relief in the shade of a tree. You feel so happy to be sitting there in the cool shade, and you start to feel calmer and more peaceful. That's an example of the result of practicing discipline: relief from the intense distress we can feel from getting caught up in our ordinary, habitual patterns.

Discipline also carries the meaning of "taking your own seat" or "standing on your own two feet." This means that you don't always need guidance from someone else like you did when you were a kid. When you were young, of course, you had plenty of authority figures. Your parents, teachers, and school counselors taught you what to do. You learned the rules for how to behave at home, in school, and in public. But once you've gone through all that, you realize that you're capable of becoming your own guide, which is a liberating realization. In the same way, on our spiritual path, we reach a point where we're capable of evaluating our own actions and correcting our own mistakes.

Ultimately, each of us is our own best judge and counselor because we know our own patterns better than anyone else. The problem with depending on teachers is that we put on our best face for them. If you're really good at it, then you can be a totally different person in their presence than you are when you walk out the door. In that case, how can a teacher really guide us? Sometimes students are even afraid of their teachers and may try to "follow the rules" or mimic excellent conduct for fear that the teacher may get upset with them. However, our training in discipline shouldn't be based on any kind of fearful thinking. That's not genuine discipline. Real discipline must come from a heartfelt desire to find our own freedom.

Ethics as Mindfulness

From one point of view, practicing discipline means following a path of ethical conduct: certain actions are to be avoided, and others are encouraged. Based on this, we might think that discipline is simply about following rules and enduring hardships. However, the primary intention of this training is to become aware of our actions, see them clearly, and be able to recognize those that are harmful and those that are beneficial. To be mindful of all our actions and take care not to cause harm to others or to ourselves is the mark of a disciplined mind. That means we have to examine our assumptions about what constitutes a positive action or a negative one. Some actions can be positive in one social context but negative in another. Discipline goes beyond just following a set of rules. It requires genuine discrimination, empathy, and honesty. Still, it's your own discipline you're developing. You're the one on the road, making your way to your own freedom.

Becoming a disciplined person means cultivating mindfulness and awareness so you can see your actions clearly and precisely. Being disciplined means you see the full picture: you see your thoughts and the intentions of those thoughts; you see how your intentions develop and are then expressed in speech or actions; and you also see the impact of your actions on yourself, on others, and on your environment. When you apply mindfulness and awareness to this whole process, you experience greater freedom. You're not limited to just repeating your habitual tendencies or blindly doing what you think you're supposed to do. You can choose whether to say what's on your mind and burning to come out, or you can pause and cool down first. That's a rebel buddha moment, when you're about to be caught again, and something steps in at the last moment and pushes you free, out of reach of disaster. That's your basic intelligence, your wakeful mind, springing into action. At first, you're more likely than not to get caught, but later, rebel buddha mind becomes so swift and precise in its actions that you can begin to relax, even when under heavy emotional fire.

It's not good enough to try being mindful and disciplined just once and then say, "Well, I tried it, but it didn't work." It takes time. You've got to try repeatedly, and then at some point, you can feel the transformative energy. Whether or not you change the way you do things, you find that the way you relate with your actions changes. If you tend to shout orders to people at work, you'll probably still do that. However, the way you relate to your shouting may be quite different.

Breaking Through Habitual Patterns

The Buddha came up with a list of ten actions that he regarded as positive, in the sense that they contribute both to an individual's development as well as to harmonious conditions within society. Of these ten, three relate to acts of the body, four to acts of speech, and three to acts of the mind. Further, he taught that when we apply mindfulness and awareness to all our actions of body, speech, and mind, we achieve something more: we start to break through the power of our habitual patterns. We disrupt their momentum as soon as we recognize that we're just repeating our usual dramas. When we become conscious of our patterns, then each time a certain habit reappears, such as a tendency to react with anger, it will be different because it won't have the same strength or sense of solidity. And as we loosen the hold of our patterns altogether, we develop a more peaceful, positive, and clear state of mind. By mindlessly indulging in these habits, however, we only deepen their hold on us.

The ten positive actions that support wakeful, compassionate living are expressed as ten things to refrain from. In terms of bodily action, discipline means realizing that it's generally harmful to kill other beings, to steal from them, or to behave inappropriately sexually. In terms of speech, we see that it's generally harmful to lie to others; to make disparaging, divisive remarks; to talk harshly; or to spend our time in meaningless gossip. And in terms of mind, we see the harm that comes from being malicious and envious, bearing grudges, and committing the error of not believing in cause and effect. This last belief is regarded as the most serious problem of all, because if we don't believe that a negative action is connected to a negative result, then we might think that we can kill, lie, and be hateful and still expect to be free, honored, and happy. That is the epitome of delusion.

We can see how this works if we look at the experience of our own mind when we engage in different types of actions. When we do something positive, like helping a friend in need, offering kind words to a stranger, or simply thinking of another person with an attitude of love and compassion, the effect on our mind tends to be calming. We feel more relaxed, open, and clear. In contrast, when we do something negative, like fight with our partner, steal from the office, or covet our neighbor's belongings, then our mind becomes more agitated, tense, and cloudy. In other words, all of our actions, whether they remain on the level of thought or are expressed in speech or bodily action, have some kind of impact on the mind.

Obviously, if we're in an environment that supports our negative habits, it's more difficult to break out of them. So it's helpful to look at our surroundings, at the culture of our home, neighborhood, or workplace.

Any tendency we may have toward harsh speech is reinforced if others around us are driven by competition and jealousy. If we're inclined to be less than truthful in money matters, to rationalize overcharging clients or cheating on taxes, then those tendencies are reinforced if the culture of our business community accepts and rewards those practices. If we've grown up in an atmosphere of intimidation and violence, then even though it isn't our natural tendency to bully others, we may fall into that behavior.

Essentially, when we're talking about discipline and ethics, we're simply talking about replacing old, self-defeating habits with new, constructive ones. There are many reasons why we do what we do, and when we look beyond our habitual patterns and environmental conditioning, we see that the underlying cause for all of it is the mind of ignorance—not knowing and not caring to know. Since we can't remedy or even see this directly at first, we begin by working to become aware of our actions. We work from the top down, or from the outside in, carrying the light of awareness with us. Eventually, a light will go on at even the deepest level of our being.

Beyond Dos and Don'ts

We must each find our own way to create a space in our life where we can concentrate on our path of individual freedom. Some people choose an environment of solitude, either literally or figuratively. They put up big signs saying, "Private property. No trespassing." You can't talk to them; you can't touch them. If you do, they remain silent and try to run away from you. It's not necessary to go that far, of course, but it's essential that we each find a certain degree of internal solitude, an undisturbed space, where we can work on our own issues and discover our personal spark, the enthusiasm that fuels our interest and keeps us going. But it's important that we don't make this into a grandiose mission, where we suddenly have to become free of everything. That's not going to happen.

We can look for freedom from whatever emotional upheaval we're going through in any moment, or we can focus on one particular habitual pattern. One of my own teachers once said, "Work with what is easiest first—the least neurotic element of your mind—and liberate that. Then work on the next one and commit to liberating that with all the strength and power of your heart." This is good advice. In this way, you accumulate single bits of your liberation like pieces of a puzzle, and when you put them all together, you find that you have complete freedom from all your habitual patterns, all your causes of suffering. On the other hand, you can, if you wish, continue to accumulate negative actions and build up your collection of confusion and suffering. It's your choice.

Again, you shouldn't take this training as a set of dos and don'ts; it's not a list of ethical demands you must meet in order to be a Buddhist. We have to remember why we are doing these things. Our purpose is simply to wake up; otherwise, we're just enforcing a prescribed code, like government regulations. I once heard about a state law that required people to register for their death certificate two weeks before they died. That's the kind of absurdity that can happen when we become so concerned with rules and policy that we forget to trust our own intelligence.

MEDITATION: GETTING TOGETHER WITH YOUR MIND

Meditation brings steadiness, calmness, and clarity to our busy, agitated mind. Without the support of meditation, it would be difficult to succeed at training in discipline. We need a focused, calm, and steady mind to see our actions clearly. By training in meditation, we become able to train in discipline.

The question here is, what are we doing in meditation? There are many different types of meditation, but the primary methods associated with the training in meditation are calm abiding meditation (*shamatha*) and clear seeing, or insight, meditation (*vipashyana*). Calm abiding meditation is sometimes called "resting meditation" or just "sitting meditation," which is what we'll call it here. It's an accurate label, because we're not doing much in this practice other than sitting and looking at the mind. Once we've learned to calm and stabilize the mind, we'll be able to practice clear seeing meditation, which brings about a deeper level of insight or direct seeing into the mind's nature. It doesn't work very well as long as the mind tends to be agitated and scatters easily. Detailed instructions for practice can be found in Appendix 1.

Whatever method you use, meditation is simply getting to know your mind. It's not about meditating "on" something or getting into a zone where you're blissfully removed from your mind's contents. Instead, the actual meaning of meditation is more like getting used to being with your own mind. Earlier, we talked about not knowing our mind—mind as the stranger in your neighborhood. Now we can look at how we can change this relationship.

Often when you want to get to know someone, you'll suggest meeting someplace for tea. You'll find a nice café, someplace quiet with comfortable seats, order your drinks, and sit down together. In the beginning, the conversation is just small talk, but as you get to know each other and feel more comfortable, an honest and open exchange starts to take place. Your new acquaintance will begin to tell you more and more about his or her life. Eventually, you start to feel that you know something about this person and what he or she is going through. You feel some connection and sympathy. You'll also have your turn to share whatever you're going through. If you want to become a good friend, however, you have to be a good listener first. You have to be fully present and let your new friend talk. If you interrupt right away and take over the conversation, then you'll never have a meaningful dialogue. Your meeting won't result in getting to know and understand each other. At a certain point, you discover that no matter how mixed up and troubled your new friend may be, you still find something genuinely good and decent within all his or her confusion.

Getting to know your mind through meditation works in much the same way. You want to know your mind on a deeper level, so you plan to spend some time together. You make a date and find a quiet place where you can sit comfortably and hang out with your new acquaintance called "my mind." In this case, your practice of sitting meditation is like the café, the place where you meet. There are nice cushions to sit on, you look at each other, and then your mind starts chattering. In fact, in the beginning, it can't stop talking. All you need to do is be a good listener. It will go on and on, telling you everything that happened in the past or that might happen in the future. But whatever it says, whether it's wisdom or bullshit, imagination or reality, all you need to do is listen.

By being there and just listening, you'll eventually learn what's going on with your mind. You'll be able to recognize its problems and come up with advice that will hit the spot. If you start diagnosing too soon, your advice will lead nowhere. If you wait to get the full story, then you can guide your mind in a direction that's productive and beneficial, one that will reduce its pain and relieve its emotional upheavals. However, knowing what will help is one thing, and getting your mind's cooperation is another. That's why developing this relationship is so important. If you saw some strange guy on the street doing something stupid and said, "Hey, you! Don't do that," do you think he would to listen to you? No, probably not. But if it was someone you knew well and you said, "Hey, friend! Please stop that," that person would be much more likely to listen to you and try his best to stop what he was doing. It's the same with our mind. If your mind is a stranger to you, and from time to time you catch it doing something negative and tell it to stop, it's not going to listen to you. But once you have developed a relationship and become friends, then your mind will be more workable, more reasonable, more amenable to change. You have a good history, and your friend will listen to you.

Just as when you make a new friend, when you develop a genuine, honest, and open relationship with your mind, you discover that in spite of everything—the anxieties, struggles, and emotional upheavals—there's something in the heart of it all that's undeniably positive. There are qualities of goodness, compassion, integrity, and wisdom that are apparent through all of your mind's confusion, and those outshine all of your mind's faults.

HIGHER KNOWLEDGE: SEEING CLEARLY

The celebrated philosopher and father of the modern scientific method, Francis Bacon, said, "Knowledge is power." *Power* implies great ability, strength, authority, and the capacity to act and accomplish our ends.

If we have power, we can use it in different ways—to control others or to exert influence on social institutions or on government itself. We can also use it for self-transformation. In this respect, we can say that spiritual knowledge is spiritual power. In the Buddhist path, we accumulate knowledge in three ways: through study, contemplation, and meditation.

First, we gain intellectual knowledge, then we personalize it through reflecting on it, and then we go beyond that to a whole new state of knowing—one that's free from reliance on reference points. That's the nature of our journey. First, we're handed a map and learn to read it; next, we're on the road but still relying on our map for directions; finally, we realize we don't need to look at the map anymore—we know it by heart. Our confidence doesn't waver, whether we're looking at the map or the road ahead; the map has dissolved into the landscape. That's higher knowledge, or one way of looking at it.

Higher knowledge might sound like something you get by attending an institution of higher learning—a spiritual graduate school. In pursuit of it, you might get to leave behind the practical concerns of everyday life in favor of an elevated, ivory-tower existence. That sounds quite nice, but here, the opposite is true. It's precisely the details and practical concerns of everyday life that make knowledge of any sort possible. And to achieve a state of higher knowledge, you need to see the details of your life extraordinarily clearly.

"Higher knowledge" here has two meanings. First, it's a way of seeing; second, it's what you see. The way of seeing here is "clear seeing," or seeing better than you usually do; seeing further and deeper than you have ever seen before. What you see (when you see this clearly) is the way things really are: when you look at yourself, you see selflessness, and when you look at the world, you see emptiness. It's like having poor eyesight for a long time and then going through a procedure that corrects the defects in your eyes. You suddenly have perfect vision, and everything appears crystal clear, without any fuzziness or distortion. The procedure you go through here to correct your vision is the training in higher knowledge that clears away your mind's confusion. Essentially, it's a process of strengthening and sharpening your natural intelligence to the point of brilliant clarity, which dispels the darkness of ignorance as it fully illuminates your mind.

At that point, the intelligence that sees and that which is seen merge in the experience of self-aware wisdom: buddha mind, awakened mind, mind that is free. The flash of insight that comes just prior to that moment is your own intelligence in action—your rebel buddha mind. At first, we rely on our intelligence simply to see our habitual patterns when they come up and not give in to them. That's the first mission of rebel buddha, which is a defensive action to keep us awake and in the game. It observes from the sidelines, stepping in from time to time. But later, our intelligence becomes more proactive and courageous; it seeks opportunities to wake us up. It goes out, engages our habitual patterns, and proclaims wakefulness in the midst of our confusion. The cause of this evolution is our training in higher knowledge, which empowers rebel buddha, our innate intelligence, to become a fully functioning force in the service of our liberation.

The meditation associated with the development of higher knowledge, or direct insight into the nature of reality, is the practice of analytical meditation. It's a conceptual form of meditation that uses logic and reasoning to investigate and analyze experience. For example, you might test your assumptions about who you are by asking yourself a series of questions: "What and where is this 'self' that I believe exists right now? Is it physical or mental? Did it exist before I was born? If not, then how could this self arise from 'no self' or from nothing? If so, then how can I say that this already existing self is 'born'?" Through this process of examination and analysis, analytical meditation exposes our confused thinking as it sharpens the intellectual power of the mind. Detailed instructions for practice can be found in Appendix 1.

Actually, we've been training in higher knowledge all along. We began clarifying our confusion the minute we asked our first question. We were cultivating our intelligence when we began to reflect on our aloneness, dissatisfaction, and suffering. Throughout the journey, we've been training rebel buddha mind to take advantage of any opening, any moment of clarity, to cut through the fog of confusion that surrounds us and binds us like a thick rope.

Mind Opened by Knowledge

The point of training in higher knowledge is not to become a container of facts or a believer in any particular philosophical system. The whole point is to clearly see what is truth and what is illusion in how we live. It means we understand the relationship of cause and effect, and we see how it functions in our life. We see that suffering is the natural result of a certain cause and that ultimately that cause is our self-clinging. We see that happiness is the result of a certain cause and that ultimately that cause is transcending our self-clinging.

When we see the truth of this, when we really get it, it has a strong impact. It wakes us up and sharpens our practices of discipline and meditation. When we don't fully appreciate this relationship, then after practicing for some time, we grow kind of tired of it and begin to ask, "Why am I doing this?" And when something unpleasant happens to us, we ask, "Why did this happen to me?" We don't even think about the vast network of causes and conditions to which we're always connected. These questions arise only when we either don't understand or forget about the principle of cause and effect. These are not just principles that sit on the pages of a book or words that come out of a teacher's mouth in a very dignified way. This is our life. This is what happens to us every day, and the situation is urgent, because life is short. If we don't take advantage of the opportunity that's in front of us in any moment—to awaken, to see, to know, to break free—then we may be giving up our very last chance.

Ordinarily, we don't question our confusion; we just go along with it. But here, we're reconnecting with our inquisitive mind, investigating what we usually take for granted. The result is a mind that's opened by knowledge, receptive to seeing beyond the bounds of what it already knows. We're cultivating our intelligence as opposed to expanding or upgrading its contents. It's like brightening a room by putting a higher-watt lightbulb in a lamp. Suddenly we can see everything in the room much more clearly.

As we go along, we can use each insight as a basis for extending our knowledge, for reaching further into the unknown. If we think, "I've got it!" at our very first "Aha!" moment, then there's no place to go from there. With that attitude, the early American pioneers might not have gotten past the Mississippi River. So we stay curious, and we keep looking. Even the most profound scientific discoveries of all time, such as the theories of Einstein, are still being investigated and revised by scientists in their own quest to understand the workings of a multidimensional reality.

The Way Liberation Begins

In sum, these are the three trainings in discipline, meditation, and higher knowledge that transform our mind from something that causes us frequent trouble and suffering into something more useful: a vehicle that will carry us to individual freedom. In the beginning, the path is very self-centered, and that is absolutely necessary. We need to focus on ourselves, see our own suffering and pain, and find our own way of working with our confusion. We also need to develop our own vision of freedom and decide on the path to our goal. It's a little bit like the corporate world, where the primary concern of the company is its own profit. As a by-product, some others may benefit, but their gain is not the company's immediate concern. Instead, the objective of a well-run company is to look after its financial health and resources, build up its market share, and get the most out of its bottom line. That's just how the path to liberation begins—by being realistic and down-to-earth, paying attention to details, and knowing clearly where you're headed.

untelling the story of self

OUR TRAINING in higher knowledge leads us first to an understanding of relative reality and then to a deeper understanding of ultimate reality: the mind's true nature of selflessness. We must see that, in the end, the root of all our suffering, all our pain, all our confusion is our own self-clinging, our sense of self-importance. That self is always causing us pain. There is no other root cause. It is just ego—that flash of "I" that's the central reference point in our personal universe. No matter what we're doing, our actions always come from and reflect back to this sense of self-consciousness. It's the starting point of duality, the splitting apart of what's naturally whole.

It's important to see, too, that the experience of "I" at its most basic level is an experience of uncertainty and fear. Why? Our sense of self isn't something that's born just once, when we're born from our parents, and continues uninterrupted our whole lives. It's born over and over. It's there, lasts only a moment, and then ceases. In a moment of not recognizing our own awareness, we experience a sense of mental darkness, an unknowingness that can be terrifying. For an instant, we have no clear sense of who we are, no reference point, no sense of direction. Then, quickly, from this state of ignorance, the notion of self is born once again—and from that, the notion of "other."

SELF AND OTHER

What is this self's relationship to this other? That's the question that the ego can never fully answer; it's always uncertain and fluctuating. Since it's born and ceases each moment, its nature is to grasp at existence.

Each time it springs into being, it creates with it a whole world that becomes its realm of power and influence. At the edge of this territory is a solid wall, a boundary seemingly impervious to doubt. Ego sits proudly at the center, ever watchful, and at the same time, ever clueless, surrounded by everything it regards as "mine": my body, my thoughts, my emotions, my values, my house, my family, my friends, and my wealth. "Other" is on the outside. Finally, ego's world is complete and in perfect balance. But in the blink of an eye, the whole thing falls apart—and in the next moment, it's back again.

When you hear something like this, what do you think? It's a strange kind of story, like a fairy tale. The question is, is it true? It's up to you to find out. When someone tells you something you don't understand or something that's very different from your own understanding, don't take it at face value. That's what the Buddha says, and that's what your mom would probably say too. You don't want to get taken advantage of or be fooled or just waste your time. Any words uttered in an authoritative voice can have the ring of truth; but the person speaking those words may not even know what he's saying. That happens a lot, in fact. Just turn on the news. But just as we can be taken in by someone else's stories, we can be fooled by the stories we tell ourselves. The greatest tale we tell ourselves, our very favorite one, is the story about who we are. However, like fairy tales, our stories are not meaningless; they're full of adventure, odd characters, symbolism, and truth. But we have to look for those meanings. Otherwise, our stories are just another entertainment.

Analytical meditation is a way of looking at the story of self by pulling it apart. It's called insight meditation because we're seeing into what we're examining at the same time. This type of meditation uses logic and reason to investigate what we think and unmask the basic assumptions we hold about ourselves and the world, assumptions we may never have thoroughly examined before. The reason for our investigation is as important as the process itself. If we forget why we're doing this practice, it can become just a mental exercise. In analytical meditation, we're looking for the truth about the cause of our suffering so we can undo it.

Meditating on Emptiness

The tradition of analytical meditation includes a number of logical reasonings that can lead us through a profound analysis of the self and the concepts that sustain our belief in it. The result is freedom from those concepts, which are based on confused thinking. It turns out that our belief in the true existence of a self is simply unreasonable.

When we reach the point of having "looked" deeply and extensively into both body and mind and are unable to find the existence of a self, we'll experience a gap. In that very moment of not finding the permanent and independent self we always assumed was there, all thinking stops. At that point, we can rest our mind in a moment of pure openness, which we call nonconceptual awareness. That's the beginning of our discovery of selflessness. We continue in this way, alternating methods of analyzing and resting.

Eventually, we'll be able to rest our mind directly in this pure openness without any preliminary analysis. It's at this point that we can say we're "meditating on selflessness." Why? Because we're resting our mind in a state of awareness in which there is no appearance of a self. Where is this self when there is no thought? While this nonconceptual awareness is always present, it's difficult to see. We're always missing it. The insight produced by clear seeing meditation, however, is known as "superior insight," which enables us to see beyond what we have previously seen. Before, we saw nothing but self-clinging, but now we see selflessness.

What the Buddha shows us in his teachings on selflessness is that we're mistaken to think there are things that exist solidly within the flow of experience that is our life. We think of who we are as something that's permanent, that continues over time in the same unchanging form, independent of external conditions. We also think that the world around us exists in the same solid way. Yet whether we look at ourselves, at objects large or small, or at the conditions of life, we don't find anything that meets those criteria. We see only change and transformation. When we apply our insight to the world around us, we see our day-to-day world in a new and brighter light. We see that the world, too, is constantly changing and has no solid core; it, too, is open, spacious, and selfless. That is a genuine glimpse of emptiness—the ultimate and true state of the mind and our world.

Treating Emptiness as Ordinary

When we talk about selflessness or emptiness, we tend to philosophize it; we make it into something so important and profound that it seems far away. We turn something in our hands into a far-fetched notion. We think of the ancient stories about yogis flying in the sky and walking through walls, and then we think of how confused we are right now. These two pictures seem miles apart. Our problem is that we associate the realization of emptiness with special individuals who have extraordinary capacities. Yet if we just shift our perspective a little, we can make it into a personal journey.

Look at it as ordinary and treat it the same way you treat everything else. The way you work with it is no different from the way you work with any other concepts you reflect on and analyze. You get to know it the way you get to know suffering and impermanence—by hanging out with it, looking at it from all sides, and letting it speak to you. When it speaks to you, you not only hear it, but you feel it as well. It becomes your personal experience. Even though you may be looking at books and using the special methods of logic and reasoning, nevertheless, you're doing it. If you don't analyze emptiness, however, if you just take as fact what the "experts" say, then it's not personal, and it's difficult to understand or bring into your experience.

When you analyze anything, you should chew it the way you chew your gum. You have to keep chewing before you taste its full flavor. In the same way, when you spend a little time examining an actual moment of experience, you begin to have a richer experience of it. When you're analyzing emptiness, for example, instead of just thinking about it, you can ask yourself, "Where is the self in this very moment? Is it in the sensation I'm feeling in my back as I sit here? Is it in the thought that's appearing to my mind right now?" Take it one step at a time, examining each experience of thought, feeling, or emotion until you actually see its selfless quality. In this way, you begin to taste emptiness. It is this taste that's important because it inspires us. It counteracts our resistance to emptiness and corrects our misunderstandings about it.

Emptiness as Fullness and Freedom

As I described earlier, the Buddhist view of emptiness is different from our usual understanding of the word. I keep coming back to this topic because it takes time and some experience of practice to develop a positive association with this concept. So long as we have only an intellectual reference point for it, emptiness sounds like nothingness, a condition of absolute deprivation, which is so far from the truth. Yet if that's our thought, we're likely to bring these ideas with us into our practice and infect it with fear. This doesn't help us to let go of our grasping so that we can actually experience its true meaning. There is no English word that can stand alone and convey the meaning of the experience of emptiness. But we can at least start with a positive concept instead of a negative one.

The terms *emptiness* and *selflessness* are meant to convey a sense of totality or fullness, which is actually experienced as a sense of openness and spaciousness. So this emptiness is not like the emptiness of an unfilled cup, a vacant room, or worse, an empty pocket. It's not like that. When we have a genuine experience of emptiness, it actually feels good. Rather than being depressed or anxious, we suddenly feel utterly carefree. It's as if we were tied up very tightly by a rope, and then someone came along and cut the rope. When we're suddenly freed from our bondage, we feel so good, so much more relaxed and happy. Similarly, we've been tied up by the rope of self-clinging for such a long time, and when we cut that rope, we experience a feeling of sheer joy at being free. It's not a vacuous place where everybody is desolate and moaning about something—that's our ordinary life.

We'll continue to miss the reality of emptiness if we remain fixated on what we think it means. That's why it's important to keep an open mind and explore the experience without any preconceived notions or judgments. We don't need to have a complete realization of emptiness in order for it to be transformative; in fact, it's said that having even a suspicion that emptiness is the nature of things will cut through the root of our confusion. So having even a little doubt about the validity of conventional reality, like thinking, "Maybe the way I've always seen myself is not the whole picture; maybe everything's not as solid as it appears," is helpful. Even that level of doubt can loosen our fixation and shake up our view of the world.

It's like a country ruled by a dictator. In the beginning, the people may believe in this person and support his ideals, but at some point, they start to wonder what he's really up to. They begin to mistrust his motives, and doubt creeps in—at that very moment, his influence weakens. He no longer has full power to rule. In the same way, when we begin to doubt the true existence of this ego-self, our habitual patterns and confusion don't have the same influence on us. Our ignorance and self-clinging can no longer enslave us the way they used to. The balance of power is changed forever.

ASKING DIRECTIONS

Once we have committed to traveling this path, we should occasionally stop and reflect on the journey. Are we still on the route we laid out for ourselves, or have we lost our way? Is the path working? Have we run into any obstacles? While we do need to stay focused on where we are and what we're presently doing, we also need to keep in mind the larger picture: where we started and where we're going. That way, we can judge where we are.

After some time, what can we expect to see? We should experience less suffering, especially in its most intense forms. Our emotions should be cooled out to some extent, and we shouldn't be completely under the control of our habitual patterns. So when we stop to review our journey, these are the signs we should look for. If they're there, then our path is on track. In general, we should feel more inquisitive, conscious, awake, and aware. Beyond that, once we've glimpsed the state of selflessness, there's a sense that we've crossed the point of no return. We can never go back to our old way of seeing. Our insights into the way mind works have given us a new perspective and greater confidence in our ability to work with our mind. It's like fresh air blowing in through the window of a small room, inviting us to enjoy the great outdoors. Yet the path is not always easy or smooth.

TRAPS AND DANGERS

There are places on any journey where the terrain can cause us to go off in a mistaken direction. Although our map is accurate, our motivation is strong, and many others have traveled this path before us, we may still find ourselves going around in circles or slipping backward. If we know where to look for the traps and dangers and confusing forks in the road, we can usually avoid getting stuck or making wrong turns.

In the beginning, our one-pointed focus on our goal of personal freedom is necessary; however, if carried to extremes, it can also lead to a kind of narrow-mindedness and sense of claustrophobia. When we start out, we may be only semi-aware of our confusion and somewhat dulled to our experiences of suffering. But as we progress, we become acutely sensitive to just how painful our suffering is. While we do need to fully experience our pain in order to be motivated to free ourselves from it, our increasing awareness of the extent and persistence of our suffering can become overwhelming. The more we feel our pain, the more we yearn to renounce it and escape from it; yet it feels inescapable.

At that point, we have two choices: we can relax into our experience, or we can freak out. If we freak out, we might start to withdraw into an increasingly narrow existence. Our intense desire to avoid being touched by anything painful might become so great that we retreat from everything—only to discover that we've become trapped in a very small space. It's like crawling into a narrow tunnel and getting stuck inside. The more anxious we become, the more we panic, and the harder it is to remember how we got there in the first place. We end up having to call the fire department to come rescue us. So when our sense of renunciation becomes too extreme, it actually produces more fear and becomes a barrier to our freedom.

We can also lose our way if we misunderstand selflessness or emptiness. When we confuse relative reality with ultimate reality, or misinterpret ultimate reality as something that destroys the conventional world, then we fall into the trap of the nihilists who see no meaning or purpose in life. Then our view of emptiness is inspired by sadness and depression, and it becomes just another tool to shut everything down. Instead of looking at the world with joy, we see it as hopeless.

If you get stuck in either of these places, you need to acknowledge it instead of struggling for a long time. When you recognize it, apply your training, ask questions, investigate—pay attention on all fronts. You never know where your liberation will come from or at what moment it will arrive. If you can't get unstuck by yourself, then you need to ask for help from someone who knows this road very well. Making that decision and asking for help are not giving up being in the driver's seat or handing the controls over to someone else. It's using your intelligence.

These are just two examples of how we can lose our way. It may be something else for you, because everyone is different. But never hesitate to ask for help or directions when you're in a jam or lost. The most effective remedy for the widest range of obstacles is the genuine experience of emptiness. But sometimes what you need is to take a break and find ways to relax your mind: seeing friends, listening to music, watching TV, or going to your favorite restaurant. And sometimes, the best thing you can do for yourself is to help someone else in need.

Getting stuck is not always a bad thing. It's an experience that may offer valuable lessons. You may see something you would otherwise have missed. Such experiences are nothing to fear. Each time you free yourself, your confidence grows. You know you can do it; you know from your own experience that on the other side of every stumbling block, there is an open road.

beyond self

ONCE WE HAVE an experience of selflessness, our confidence grows. As our solid sense of self begins to dissolve, the boundary separating self and other naturally starts to dissolve as well. We discover that we're no longer on the other side of a thick wall, cut off from the world. When we connect this new sense of openness with our original dedication to personal liberation, we discover that we can be full participants in the life of the world, even as we leave our ego-clinging and self-centered perspective behind.

We can see now that the trip is transforming the traveler. Our path, at this point, becomes less about traveling to a destination that we call "liberation" and becomes more a way of life. We no longer focus solely on how to get out of our own personal suffering. It may come as a surprise to us, but by studying our mind, we discover our heart; by freeing our mind, we open our heart; and our vision of freedom naturally expands to include others. Instead of seeking to protect ourselves from confusion and chaos, we begin to appreciate that confusion as being full of opportunities to train our mind further. The possibilities are actually infinite. For that reason, we feel a sense of delight at being in the world and working with others; it never becomes tiring. Our budding experience of selflessness opens a door to a new sense of appreciation for the full range of human experience.

This sense of delight that comes along with our newly found appreciation is basically an aspect of desire—the very thing we've been working so hard to overcome. The problem with desire up to this point has been that it has always been bound up with clinging and self-interest. When this clinging lets up, desire transforms into energy that connects us to others. Its qualities of warmth, interest, and enthusiasm are still present, but it's no longer so blind or impulsive. Because it's not purely interested in its own gratification, there is the potential for generosity, kindness, and compassion. This selfless expression of desire is gentler and more open than our neurotic version of it. So desire is no longer a big problem for us.

TAMING AND TRAINING AGGRESSION

After working with desire, what we have to work with next is aggression, which is one of the most destructive mental states and our biggest problem now. When we think of aggression, we normally think of something that's obviously violent: an outburst of anger where somebody is cursing and kicking a garbage can. That, of course, is a superficial level of aggression that's easy to identify and control. More problematic are our deeper levels of aggression, because they're more difficult to see and work with. Nevertheless, a mind of anger, whether overt or hidden, always cuts off communication and makes us insensible to the feelings of others. So when we speak of aggression here, we're talking both about an underlying mental state that's going on in our minds all the time, as well as about specific physical or verbal acts of anger.

There is a great deal of passive aggression in our culture. You may be carrying around an attitude of hostility and grievance without once raising your voice or hand in anger. Sometimes it comes out in your need to prove something to somebody. If somebody says something to you that hurts your pride or intimidates you, then you might feel like you have to somehow push back. If you catch yourself writing long e-mails to that person, going on and on to prove your point—that's aggression. There's nothing wrong with wanting to be clear, but when you become obsessive about explaining yourself, you've entered the realm of aggression. That can lead you down the path to outright anger, even if you were just irritated in the beginning.

It's only through seeing our aggression and working with it consciously that we can begin to open our hearts. And that's the whole point of our path now. We're no longer alone, contemplating our own personal suffering and working out our individual freedom in private. Once we have seen through our self-clinging, our eyes are open wider. We see not just the spot in front of us that calms our mind and brings our busy thoughts to rest, but all the way to the horizon. Now we see the fullness, energy, and play of a very large world. We realize that, without giving up on our goal of personal liberation, we can reach out to others and include them in our aspiration for freedom and our commitment to achieving it. So in the same way that we worked with desire, we now work with our anger, which is still untamed and untrained to some degree. We bring mindfulness and awareness to our angry thoughts and feelings and the ways we act those out. We also contemplate our anger, analyze it, and try to see its selfless quality.

There is a direct connection between selflessness and compassion. These two experiences are the keys to the rest of our journey, and each becomes more powerful as the other strengthens. Although we can work on them separately, we can't really separate them or the effects they have on us. We discover that the more we open our hearts, the more we appreciate our own mind, confusion and all. And the more we appreciate our mind, the more we appreciate others and the richness of the world, confusion and all. This is how we find joy in our everyday life.

No Piece of Cake

When we speak of training, we're talking about training rebel buddha, who is with us until buddha appears alone. We're in the process of awakening until we're awake, then there's no more process, no more journey. We are where we want to be. Our focus up until now has been on accumulating knowledge, developing our insight, and applying that to our life. This is how we have been training our mind, strengthening its power to free us. However, rebel buddha is not all mind and clear thinking. Rebel buddha has a very large heart with desires and passions of its own: a desire for personal freedom and a passion for the freedom and happiness of others. That heart needs training too. When those passions and insights come together, we look at the world with a single vision. There are opportunities everywhere to accomplish the aims of both mind and heart; in fact, those opportunities are the same. There is no longer any reason to think of "my spiritual path" and "my ordinary life" as different or separate. They become one path, one way of life.

The training we go through now is primarily training in reducing our selfishness—the opposite of selflessness. So we work with methods to let go of our attachment to thinking only of ourselves and our own benefit. It's like we've been only children for a long time, but now we have many siblings and relatives of all kinds and must learn how to share our toys. The reason we have not been able to share—to feel equal concern for the happiness and freedom of others—is because of our fixation on ourselves. We've been focused on "me" for so long that it's not easy to give up this orientation. It's no piece of cake. However, our previous training has sharpened our eyesight so we can see the possibility of letting go of our self-obsession.

Now our current training makes it even sharper. We begin to see selflessness wherever we look—not only in our own minds, but also in the minds of others and in the world itself. All thought, all emotion, all concepts have the same quality of openness. None of it is solid. Instead of a world fixed by thought, pinned down by our notions of this and that, we see a world at play, changing moment by moment. This way of seeing, called "twofold selflessness," brings a panoramic view of ultimate reality. The perception of selflessness that applies only to this "I" is like looking at the ocean from a nice beach house window. You see the ocean, but just a part of it. It may be from a distance or at an angle. Real estate agents and hotel managers call this a "partial ocean view." In contrast, the experience of twofold emptiness is like standing on a cliff at Big Sur with nothing in any direction to obstruct or limit your view. You see the full sweep of ocean, sky, and landscape stretching out before you. That's the difference between the view of individual selflessness and twofold selflessness; one is partial and one is complete.

Selfless Heart

The two qualities that are marks of our journey at this point are immense insight into selflessness and immense compassion. And although the two are equally important, we must have a strong sense of selflessness in order for our compassion to be genuine. Without that knowledge, our desire to help others is always mixed with self-interest. Even when we do good deeds, we often have a hidden agenda, such as an expectation of gratitude or compliance with our views when we give gifts, advice, or an offer of help. When we can approach the practice of compassion with some genuine knowledge of selflessness, our attitude won't be particularly goal-oriented or have a hidden agenda. We won't be going around trying to save people, as if we were going to be awarded a gold medal bearing the inscription Number One Liberator for our troubles. That's a very theistic approach, but sometimes we see it even in Buddhism, especially where Buddhism has been influenced by theistic traditions. But here, we're simply being in the world, learning to live a life that is inspired by wisdom and compassion, trying to be as helpful to others as we can.

We can look at the life of Marpa, one of Tibet's greatest teachers, as an example. He was an excellent farmer and businessman, a "householder yogi," as they say. Although he possessed a treasury of the Buddha's teachings and mastery of all of them, he never went out seeking students or trying to convert anyone. Those students who came to him had to ask again and again to be taught. It was difficult to get help from Marpa. Yet he's one of the most important and revered figures in Tibetan Buddhism, because he had the great wisdom to know exactly which teachings would be helpful to which students. He didn't give anything beyond that. So his teachings were always effective and nothing was wasted.

If we think that the Buddhist view of practicing compassion is going around saving the unenlightened, then that's no different from the view of the religious sects whose members knock on our doors, bringing the "good word" to us right in our homes. They're trying to save us from our sins, and that's a very kind gesture. But that's not how we should try to benefit people; we're not trying to save anyone with our little Buddhist trip. Our trip or spiritual journey here is simply leading a way of life with intelligence and compassion and bringing benefit to people through the natural expression of those qualities.

WINDOWS OF OPPORTUNITY

Before we can extend our compassion to others, we first have to extend it to ourselves. How do we do this? We have to look at our own mind and appreciate how our own neurotic expressions—our confused thoughts and disturbing emotions—are actually helping us wake up. Our aggression can help us develop clarity and patience. Our passion can help us let go of attachments and be more generous. Basically, once we see that this mind of confusion is also our mind of awakening, we can appreciate it and have confidence in our ability to work with it. It's a good mind after all, the mind that will carry us to enlightenment. When we understand this, we can begin to let go of our previous attitude of revulsion toward our emotions.

First, we regarded our emotions as negative, something to overcome; we needed to cool out, calm down. Now we see how the very energy of emotions sparks our intelligence and encourages us to wake up, so we can appreciate how they help us to see more clearly. We begin to understand what they've been telling us all along. We've been sitting around listening to our mind, letting it speak, getting to know this stranger, and now we've clicked into another level in our conversation. We not only hear our friend's words, we also feel the warmth or coolness of their emotional temperature. We have a more intimate and heartfelt exchange because the connection and trust are there.

Anger is not just being mad about something. Passion is not just desire to have something. They aren't just habitual patterns or afflicted states of mind. Within them, there is an urge for clarity, a longing for genuine connection, the desire for freedom. Instead of being "the enemy," our emotions are actually the face of rebel buddha. We haven't seen her face before; we haven't seen what he might look like walking around in the ordinary world. Up until now, rebel buddha has been the sharpness of the sword of our intelligence. Now we see that rebel buddha is also the softness of our heart. It's so soft, it can't ever be completely broken, which means it's also tough. In a sense, our emotions and confused thoughts are staging their own revolution of mind all the time. They're resisting our unfair, repressive treatment of them.

They're saying, "Don't freeze my energy; don't cover me with labels; don't try to improve me. Be a little braver. See me and accept me for what I really am. You might be surprised."

Once we begin to recognize the positive potential inherent in mind's confusion, we can appreciate this mind of ours instead of seeing it as just a problem. If we can look at our own mind more positively, with this sense of appreciation, then there is no way not to appreciate the world. But if we can't appreciate our own neurosis, then there's no way to appreciate the world, which is full of neurotic people. Like it or not, that is our world.

So the next step is appreciating the helpfulness of the neuroses of others. Their confusion, their emotions, their suffering can also wake us up. They impact our mind and touch our heart at once. If we can genuinely relate to our neurosis and their neuroses at the same time, every meeting, every exchange becomes mutually liberating. This attitude is the key to working with other people. It's what makes it possible and what gives us the desire to do it in the first place. If we look at others with a judgmental, suspicious, or annoyed state of mind before we even talk to them, then we're closing our window of opportunity for working with them. There isn't much we can do at that point. If we want nothing to do with confusion and neurotic people, then we can try to run away from the world again. We can see if it's possible to run away from our own mind and all our relationships with others.

We can go into a solitary retreat, of course, and leave the chaos and confusion of New York or Seattle behind. But when we're planning for our retreat, our actions are sometimes puzzling. Little by little, we start to bring more of the world with us. We have to make sure that the retreat cabin has an Internet connection for our laptop. We have to remember to bring our cell phone charger, energy bars, and vitamin water. And we know we can't get good coffee once we're there, so we have to make sure to pack all our coffee supplies. We may want to bring our portable espresso machine. Soon we're taking a whole Starbucks with us when we're supposedly trying to run away from it all. No matter how hard we try to run away from the world, we always bring the world with us. Even if we were to forego all these material gadgets, we would bring the world with us in the form of our vivid memories and projections, concepts and emotions, hopes and fears. Our little retreat cabin in the wilderness would barely be able to accommodate such a vast array of characters. And all their scenarios would disturb our peace and keep us up at night just like the sirens in the big city.

No matter how bad it looks or how horrible it may feel at times, this mind we have right now is our only hope for awakening. It's our only asset, our capital savings. It's the only thing we have on which to stake our freedom. Whatever we've been depositing into the bank account of our mind over the course of our lifetime has been drawing interest to the point where we're now pretty rich with it, whatever it may be. We may be holding a portfolio of anger or jealousy, or it may be more diversified and mixed with empathy and love. And so it is for everyone. We can only come across the experience of wakefulness with this mind we have, rich as it is with neurotic emotions of all kinds. And we can only work with others by connecting with the minds they have, which will be equally rich with confusion.

Expect Neurotic People

If you're sincere in your desire to work with others, you should expect neurotic people and be willing to work with their confusion. You should not expect, in the beginning, to connect with others on the basis of their sanity or awakening mind alone. If you're looking only for reasonable, pleasant people to help, those with a clear sense of equanimity, wisdom, and compassion, you won't find many opportunities. The people who possess such qualities may not want your help and may not appreciate your enthusiasm for saving them. When you do have an opportunity to help another person, it is usually because you've found a way to connect to his or her confusion.

You may run into people on the street who are habitually aggressive, always drunk, or just totally confused in some way. Or you may routinely meet such people in more familiar places—your home, office, or seats of high power. These encounters always raise questions about how to connect with someone in a way that allows genuine communication. You have to approach each person individually. Because people are different, there is no single way. You have to try to see the particular habits of thought and emotion that dominate their lives, and appreciate their unique neurotic "signature." You can't just jump in and start giving advice. You need to be discriminating and examine the situation, like Marpa, to see what will help. There's no need to offer something that helps you or helped your Aunt Mary but won't help someone else.

When you realize, for example, that a woman in your office has issues with anger and is difficult for everyone to deal with, what do you do? First, appreciate that she's caught up in a pattern of confusion and that her confusion causes her more pain than it's causing you, because it touches all parts of her life. You're only dealing with it at the office. Second, remember that anger is a habit, and even strong habits are workable. Then, with an open mind, look for some window of opportunity to make a personal connection. It's like finding a soft spot in a wall of aggression and anxiety through which you can enter your coworker's world. Once you're inside her world, you can have a genuine conversation. There's more trust, because you both feel that you're on the same side. That doesn't mean that you share exactly the same perspective, only that both of you can honestly share your perspectives without blame and labeling. Whatever happens, it's a start.

This in no way implies that, on our path, we should assume the role of therapist or try to guide anyone through a therapeutic process. However, we can offer support, understanding, and genuine kindness without judgment or expectation. In this way, we meet a mind disturbed by aggression with a mind of clarity and compassion. Such a meeting can initiate a shift of perspective or change of heart, whether that's in the near or distant future.

Making and Avoiding Meaningful Connections

When you're trying to communicate with someone, the labels you use to identify each other can either help or hurt. Some labels are neutral, like *book* or *tree* or *pencil*. Other labels that you might think of as being neutral can actually be loaded with meaning for someone else and convey a sense of judgment. Moreover, the same label coming from the mouths of different people can have entirely different meanings. For example, if

I said to you, "I'm a spiritual person, and you're a worldly person," what would you think? And if you said the same thing to me or someone on the street, what would you mean by it?

We're often quick to label people as being either spiritual or worldly types. People on the street are as likely to do this as meditators in shrine rooms; moreover, culturally traditional presentations of the dharma can serve to support this sense of contrast. However, such sharp distinctions actually close the window of opportunity to communicate with others. The moment we label someone as *worldly* and they, in turn, label us as *spiritual,* our communication stops right there, along with any possibility of developing a deeper relationship.

We avoid this distinction when we relate to our path as simply a way of life rather than a journey to a reach certain goal or state of accomplishment, where we're saving people along the way. Instead, our journey becomes our life itself, and our practice is relating with everyday situations as they manifest and play out in our minds and emotions and in the minds and emotions of others. When you operate on such a fundamental level, there is a natural flow of communication between you and your world. When you talk to your neighbors using the language and experience of everyday life, they will understand you. Mention anger or jealousy or passion, and you'll have an interested audience. Many people would be open to hearing how you work with these emotions—and all the rest of the seven deadly sins—in your life.

On the other hand, if you leave that level and start speaking like a scholar or a high priest, not many people on the street will understand you or care about what you're saying. You can connect more directly and personally with others if you're simply sharing common experiences of working with your life and not particularly discussing spirituality. That's why it's sometimes easier to connect with people in bars or smoking on the sidewalk than with people in a shrine room. If you don't believe me, look at those people you meet in airport terminals handing out religious tracts and photos of their holy leaders; they're generally avoided like the plague.

When we do make a genuine connection with another person, it's a heart connection. We can touch another heart, another life, only with our own heart and life. We may be the ones to benefit most; you never know what will happen or who will end up liberating whom. When we reach out, we're offering to let go of our own preconceptions about "who I am," "who you are," and what could or should happen. A meeting of minds or hearts is never about just one person; it's like a chemical reaction, an alchemy that can transform both.

Nothing to Lose

Our appreciation for this crazy, confused world comes from realizing that we can wake up with the mind we have right now. This more positive perspective toward our thoughts and emotions doesn't mean that we indulge our habitual patterns, but that we make the best use of them. When anger strikes, we can use its brilliant energy to see the whole pattern of anger more clearly and cut through it. And all of our experiences can help spark our insight in the same way. Eventually, we'll cut through ignorance at its very root. This discovery of the workability of our mind is cause for joy. It's what makes it possible for us to love our world just as it is. Instead of striving so hard toward a goal, we can begin to relax and enjoy the process.

If the only thing life had to offer was an endless cycle of pain and pleasure, then yes, go off to a mountaintop or enter a monastery and find some peace of mind. After all, we don't want to make our home on a battleground or live every day in a madhouse. We may enjoy watching the madness and drama of the human condition on TV, but we don't really want our life to be an action movie, a melodrama, or a reality show. But in spite of all our complaints and judgments, instead of running away from the world, we find that we're drawn back into the thick of it again and again. Our passion for this life comes from appreciating both its challenges and opportunities, and also from realizing that, in the end, we have nothing to lose by opening our heart. We're stuck here with this mind anyway, and there's nothing much we can do about it. We can't throw it away and purchase an upgraded model.

As long as we're stuck in this world with this mind, why not make the best use of it? Why not just find a way to enjoy ourselves, like when we were kids and the teacher put us in study hall? We knew we couldn't escape, but we usually found a way to entertain ourselves. Even a piece of paper could become an airplane to carry a message across the room—or carry out an aerial attack on the teacher. Whether we are little kids in a monastery wanting to go outside to play, adults in lockdown at a prison, executives in a board meeting, or astronauts orbiting the earth, we're all in the same boat. As long as we're here, we might as well learn from the child we once were and get creative.

10

the altruistic heart

SOMETIMES WE SAY it's a big world, and sometimes we say it's a small world. Whichever way we think of it, we know there are countless people on this earth and as many kinds of suffering as there are inhabitants of the planet. Whether suffering comes from outside or from within, it's often made worse by the sense of isolation and aloneness it brings with it. Suffering gives us the feeling of having no friends. When we open our heart to others, the magnitude of the suffering we meet can be overwhelming. Our sense of love and compassion can go into a state of shock. It's helpful, then, to remember that sometimes the most powerful medicine we can offer for suffering of any kind is simply kindness. It says, "You're not alone. I see you; I hear you; I'm with you." Even if it's only for a moment or a day, that sense of genuine connection can change the trajectory of a life. To be genuine and kind is like a broad-spectrum remedy for the pain that afflicts the heart. Giving food, shelter, and work are important, and that should always be done too, as much as possible. If you're in a position to give any of those, don't withhold them. But every one of us is in a position to be genuine and kind.

To offer this kindness to others, we first have to learn to be kind toward ourselves. Then we can approach others and extend that same kindness to them. Again, wanting to help others doesn't mean we have the goal of saving them, in the sense of setting them on the "right course" according to our view. If there's any way we can really save someone, being genuine and kind is probably the only way. You're not going to save people by pushing them toward a goal you have in mind for them. If you're driven by such a motivation, then your actions are more like those of a religious missionary than a best friend. There's a lot of ego-centricity in wanting to be a savior, and it's a theistic view as well. You may be thinking, "I just want to save Joe and Mary from themselves. I'm not trying to save their souls." In that case, you may be using a different label, but your attitude and actions are much the same.

You could, instead, be like a best friend to others. When you have a best friend, you know that person will always try to be there for you when you need help. Your friend isn't there trying to convert or save you, only to give you support and create whatever environment you need. A relationship can go wrong when one person tries to save the other. You may be trying to rescue a friend or partner from grief, depression, or simply the misfortune of holding the wrong political views; neverthe-less, you must respect the integrity of each individual and your own limitations of knowledge. On the other hand, in many cases, kindness is all you can offer—and all you need to offer. A kind, good, and gentle heart can melt the barriers that separate us. When you feel the quality of genuine kindness in your own heart and can extend that to another person, then although that person may be in a sad or difficult situation, your kindness can convey a healing sense of warmth and peace.

Our sense of appreciation for this world that brings us so much suf-fering and joy is just the beginning of a greater adventure. Once both heart and mind are opened and joined and working together, we become more bold and daring. We move forward on a path that leads us from an outlook of appreciation to one consisting solely of altruism. We can't do this all at once, of course. It's something we develop by working with our habits step-by-step. If we get into the habit of appreciating others, then that habit will become stronger. If we also get into the habit of looking at the world through the lens of selflessness, then that habit will become stronger too. Together these habits will transform an attitude of self-interest into a compassionate and unselfish concern for others.

Are compassion and altruism different? From a Buddhist perspec-tive, they are the same. Technically, however, altruism seems to mean that our sense of compassion expands to the point where we become devoted to the welfare of others. That doesn't mean we don't care for ourselves at the same time, but in practice, we tend to think of what someone else might need or want before we think of our own needs and desires. If we're eating a meal with others, we naturally offer the main dish to each person before serving ourselves. If we're on a waiting list for an operation, we don't try to jump to the head of the line. If there's someone with a more urgent need than ours, we let them go ahead of us. When it comes to power and money, we're happy to see it in the hands of anyone who uses it wisely, for the good of all, whether that is ourselves or someone else. In other words, genuine altruism comes from a state of equanimity. We're at peace with ourselves and content with what we have. Having overcome self-fixation, we're relaxed and happy. Giving is effortless and a source of joy.

LOVE'S ADVENTURE

While this looks good on paper, it's also somewhat unbelievable. Are such idealistic portrayals even helpful if you don't know anyone who actually lives up to them? Perhaps the point is that you see in yourself moments of such compassion and complete selflessness. You have people whom you love unconditionally. You have times when you even love yourself. There are hours or days when you feel at peace, and your actions are gentle and kind. In this sense, you already have an altruistic heart. You don't need a new or better heart. You need only to recognize the heart you have and work with it, believe in it, and challenge it until it regains its state of full power. That is the adventure your rebel buddha is happy to go on.

This basic seed of compassion is present at all times in the minds of all beings—whether human, animal, or any other kind of creature that may be out there. No matter how horrible a person may be, this seed of compassion will manifest in some form in his or her life. Yes, there are ruthless, callous tyrants, past and present, who have wreaked havoc on the world and caused incalculable suffering. And there are people who trade the happiness and welfare of their families and friends for some measure of wealth, power, or fame every single day. We look at someone like this and think, "Surely this person is hopeless." We see no spark of decency, no wholesomeness, no honesty in that person.

That's how far we can fall from grace, so to speak. We can almost lose our connection to our awakened nature. Yet deep in the heart of even the most corrupt or primitive of beings, there's still a basic sense of compassion. There's something to connect to. No one is hopeless. There's a quality of softness, a potential for gentleness, a sense of vulnerability that they're usually afraid of showing. Maybe it's that they fall in love or have a passion for music or art, but there's always something that reveals a connection to their humanity. Even the most ferocious animal predators that eat their prey alive will tenderly nurture their own young.

This seed of compassion, this sense of openness, softness, and warmth is what we need to connect with now. The more genuine we can be, honest with ourselves and without pretension or guile in relation to others, the more aware we become of all the potentiality that exists around us. The world becomes more brilliant, more surprising and fresh, and even more endearing. On this journey, it's natural to fall in love with the world. In spite of its suffering and its dizzying confusion, it's also a world of great beauty and power that nurtures and sustains us on many levels. That's why we create art and enjoy it; it's the reason we sing and dance, play games, tell stories, and wonder why an apple falls from a tree at a certain rate. We create problems, to be sure, and then we try to solve them, which we sometimes do. We're a work in progress.

Compassion or altruism, then, is not about being perfect or just doing good; it's about this daring heart that cherishes others and life itself. We may never save the world, but our actions do help in profound ways because they arise spontaneously from love. That may sound like a romantic notion, because we have this idea that love is blind. It can be irrational and impractical. But our deep feeling for the world can also generate further wakefulness rather than obscuring our vision and power of reason. When we're guided by intelligence, our actions are not impulsive. A genuinely spontaneous action is skillful; it is precise and appropriate, takes in the whole context, and moves situations in the direction they should go. Regardless of our intention, an action is not actually compassionate if it doesn't help.

To fall in love in this sense is not necessarily easy. We would have to be pretty stupid not to realize this. So it's better to think about how we can bring this heart of compassion into our life in a practical way. Each of us will have subtle differences in how we do it. What's best for me may be different from what's best for you. This is a very personal, inner journey. We're bringing heart and mind ever closer together, toward the state of joyful union. We're closing the gap between spiritual and mundane, up and down, self and other. This is the way we transform our path from a problem to be solved or a goal to be attained into a way of life that's genuinely meaningful and beneficial. At the same time, we can't be certain who or what we'll meet along the way, so it's also an adventure.

The Grant Application

Imagine if we went up to someone and said, "I'd really like to help you, but first you need to clean up your act a little bit. And it would be great, too, if you'd be a little nicer to me. Then, yes, I think I could be a big help to you." We may not actually say this out loud or even be fully conscious of it, but that kind of precondition is sometimes there. That's where our confusion lies in terms of extending our heart of compassion. We want to help people, but at the same time, we have our own requirements they need to meet first. It's like applying for a grant from a charitable foundation. There are pages of prerequisites, conditions, and obligations to meet and promises to keep before you get the foundation's support. That's not really the vision of compassion we're talking about. Compassion here begins with a sense of acceptance. It's more of a handshake approach than a prenuptial agreement. We meet and make a connection, and then we work out the details as we go along.

Facing Real-World Challenges

If we're able to set aside our list of requirements and accept others as they are, then we can find an intelligent way to connect with their mental or emotional state and actually be helpful. When we get to this point, our compassion is genuine; it's not contrived or specialized—reserved for some and withheld from others. As our life becomes increasingly infused with this altruistic outlook, our path and life begin to intersect and eventually become one. Then there is little distinction between what we call our spiritual path and our ordinary life. When our neighbors see us, they don't see a religious figure or even, necessarily, a spiritual one. They don't see a recluse or monk who adheres to an otherworldly code of conduct. They simply see a good neighbor. When life and spiritual practice blend in this way, then everything we meet in our day-to-day life can be part of our practice. Nothing needs to remain outside of our journey.

However, because there's no longer any sharp contrast between life and practice, how do we know if we're really practicing? Here we are, in our comfortable house with our partner, kids, little dog, little kitty, or piglet in the backyard. That's pretty much the way we were before we began our journey. If we were members of a monastic community, on the other hand, we would be living within a distinct environment with a set schedule and code of conduct that constantly reminded us of our intention to practice. Everything would be laid out clearly. Since that's not the case for us, what is the source of our discipline? It's the mindfulness and awareness we developed earlier. As householders, we provide our minds, as opposed to our lifestyle, with a sense of discipline. So the question, are we really practicing? is one we must each answer for ourselves.

Look at your mind when you wake up in the morning and discover that there's no milk for your coffee, it's raining again, the car needs gas, and your kids have their headphones on and are refusing to speak to you. In that moment, where is your equanimity, your compassion? If you need reminders that will urge you toward practice, you can easily find them in your own life.

As householders, we have many more opportunities to face real-world challenges than hermits or renunciants do. The time we spend initially working with our own minds is preparation for meeting those challenges, for bringing our mind training into action in the world. For example, we might practice working with our emotions in meditation. We start by sitting quietly and then we invite our anger or jealousy to come, so we can look at it and work with it. This kind of training is extremely important, but it's also a bit like the field exercises or war games practiced in the military. Although it provides us with basic skills and strategies for recognizing and working with our emotional states, we are nevertheless still in a kind of demilitarized zone (DMZ) where we're protected from enemy fire. We're safe as long as we're in our own little cocoon. Eventually we need to come out of hiding to test our skills and see what we've learned. We have to be out in the open and risk the dangers of real anger, real jealousy, real desire—to go beyond being a trainee, a Buddhist cadet. It is in the arena of your own life that you become a warrior and win your freedom.

How Far Are You Willing to Go?

Once we join practice with day-to-day life, every corner of our world offers us a way to explore wakefulness, whether we're in a shrine hall or on the street. Therefore, we have to keep checking our minds, looking at our motivations in every situation. Although we're not trying to "save" the masses of humanity, by making use of these everyday opportunities, our whole life becomes a path toward freedom that contributes to the freedom of others at the same time.

This noble, selfless heart of compassion that we're talking about may sound extreme. Give up all self-interest? Dedicate yourself 100 percent to the welfare of others? And keep in mind, we're talking about actual people, not just an abstraction of "others." These charming or irritating people may live on Main Street or Wall Street. They may get their news from Comedy Central or the Fox News Network. They may be clever and insightful or stupid and intolerable. How far are you willing to go from your baseline of opinion and values to reach out to someone who's confused and suffering?

In fact, compassion is not a state that we manufacture in order to accomplish good works for someone else's benefit. It's part of our nature, our basic being, and when we connect with this nature, we're enriched and benefited at least as much as the person who is the object of our sympathy and concern. When we're genuinely engaged in a process of working with others, we're automatically working with ourselves as well. So any moment we spend in such a process is not wasted, even from the point of view of individual freedom. There is a Buddhist saying: "Helping others is the supreme way to help yourself." Right when we're in the midst of trying to counsel another person, giving it our all, really trying to help by offering our best insights into their problems, that's when we might have a sudden insight into a problem of our own. It's often in our efforts to help others in their confusion that we can experience some kind of liberation of our own confusion. That potential for mutual benefit is always there. For that reason, we shouldn't hold the view that we're the clever ones and this poor, confused guy in front of us doesn't know anything. At the same time, don't expect any particular result or payoff on either side. Genuine compassion, in a nutshell, is uncontrived.

Fearlessness

Compassion can evolve from something small and specific into something as vast as the sky. We may start with a simple sense of appreciation for a piece of art or for our pet and find that we're gradually opening our hearts and appreciating more of our world. If we don't hold back from this process, then our sense of appreciation and empathy can expand to encompass the entire world and each and every person in it. But first we have to be willing to open our heart. That very willingness can then evolve all the way into a state of fearlessness. Why do we need to be fearless in order to go where we're going? Because when we open our heart, we expose who we are to the world. We don't open our heart only in private, behind closed doors. It's an act of courage to be who we are in any situation, without retreating behind a barrier. Although it may sound contradictory, we can actually be vulnerable and fearless at the same time.

This kind of vulnerability is sometimes misunderstood as weakness instead of an expression of strength. In ordinary terms, being open could mean that we're defenseless, at risk of being attacked. It would follow, then, that without some kind of defensive system in place, we're inviting trouble. This is so ingrained in us that we often react defensively even when we don't know what we're protecting; it may simply be our neurosis. Nevertheless, this shield of defense must come down on the spiritual journey, and the only way we can really do that is by trusting ourselves. In this case, trusting ourselves means that we not only trust that we can work effectively with our own neurosis, but also that we can work with the neuroses coming at us. Then the whole environment becomes workable. When we lose sight of this view, then the whole thing feels oppressive and there's no real sense of opening.

To be fearless doesn't mean that we become more aggressive, solidify our self-fixation, or increase our self-importance. It simply means that we're willing to be open, genuine, and truthful with ourselves and others. If we can do that, then there's nothing to fear. If, however, we are putting up a façade of being a good and helpful person and concealing an agenda of self-interest, then there will always be a reason to hide and something to fear. As long as our intentions are pure, as long as our vision is clear, as long as we stand on the ground of trust, there's nothing to worry about. Once we have ticked off those check boxes, we just need to relax.

From Awakening to Awakened: Cause and Result

In Western cultures, we might say that we fall in love with our heart and out of love with our head. Heart is for feeling and head is for rational thought, right? If that's the case, then there are two seats of power within us that are not always in agreement. However, from a Buddhist perspective, the true seat of the mind is the heart—not the brain or head. Compassion and clear awareness are naturally together, and when we connect with this experience in a deep and genuine way, it's described as giving rise to "awakened heart" or "awakened mind." Either way, if we say heart or mind, it means the same thing. It is awakened being, pure presence that is naturally open, completely aware, and unconditionally loving. The quality of awakened heart, as we'll call it, exists in "seed" form in all our experiences of mind.

What helps us to transform our potential from its seed form into the state of full blossoming is, like everything else, a matter of cause and effect. If we plant a seed in good soil, water it, ensure that sunlight reaches it, and so forth, the seed will ripen and eventually produce a mature plant with flowers and fruit. In the same way, there are causes that support the full awakening of our heart. A cause is something that has the power to produce a specific result, so what we want to know is, what are the causes that have an awakening power?

The Buddha taught that the experience of awakened heart can be brought about in five ways:

By relying on qualified spiritual friends

By cultivating the qualities of loving-kindness and compassion

By increasing your positive actions

By studying the teachings and sharpening your intellect

By mixing the knowledge you gain through study with your mind[1]

Except for the first one, we've been discussing these all along. Basically the prescription is to make the best use of the opportunities we have in this short life.

Now since it's traditional and recommended to have something called a "teacher," it's time to look at this concept, which is among the most interesting, misunderstood, and at times controversial of all the transformational powers of the Buddhist path.

There are different kinds of teachers you can have at different stages of your path. These may be different people or the same person taking different roles. One type of teacher is the philosopher-scholar, someone who can instruct you in the basic teachings and fundamentals of the path. Another type is the teacher who can act as a guide for you and advise you on how to put those fundamentals into practice. When you run into obstacles, he or she can help you work through them. Then you have the teacher who is more of a "wise person," who can point you to the door to deeper knowledge and show you how to walk through it. So the first teacher is like a law professor, who is an expert theoretician and can teach you the basic rules and explain their history and the reasoning behind them. The second is like a lawyer, who knows how that theory works in real life and not just in textbooks. The third is like a judge, the most painful but necessary teacher of all, who will point out your weak spots and keep you honest.

These are generalizations, of course. Your teacher may appear in any form. Nevertheless, the Buddha taught that the ultimate teacher we should rely on is our own nature of mind. But until we meet that "inner" teacher in a clear way, these other teachers can help us and prevent us from turning our experience of selflessness back into a solid ego.

WHO IS THE TEACHER?

We're accustomed to a certain way of understanding what *teacher* means because of all our past experiences with schools and teachers—from our first trip to kindergarten all the way up to our years at a university or vocational school. That, however, is not really the meaning of the word used by the Buddha when he first introduced the idea of what we call "teacher." The word he used meant "spiritual friend." It's important to reflect on what we mean today when we say "teacher," especially in a spiritual sense. It is of more consequence than we might imagine, because when misunderstood, the teacher-student relationship can become very heavy and kind of depressing.

In our educational system, we may view teachers of small children as surrogate nannies, but as children grow physically and intellectually, we tend to regard their teachers with a special respect. We trust that the teachers are knowledgeable in their field and that their motivations are benevolent. The higher the level of schooling, the more respect we're ready to bestow, but at the same time, we may be less able to relate with them from the perspective of common ground. What do you say to a professor of high-energy astrophysics or the poetics of Aristotle? We might feel that there's an unbridgeable gulf between us and such an erudite, learned person, whose thoughts are occupied by such lofty subjects. This sense of disparity can be even more pronounced in the spiritual arena, where we place "holy" figures on a pedestal, far above the sphere of ordinary men and women—almost to the point where we regard them as a higher order of being. At a certain point, it becomes impossible to bridge that gap. Then there's no possibility for either party to communicate genuinely. Each person has a recognized and fixed position and role in the relationship: one is superior, and the other is inferior. One is all-knowing, and the other is an empty vessel, a supplicant, a beggar for knowledge and wisdom and blessings.

In the absence of any actual connection, the gap between student and teacher becomes filled with projections. The student thinks, "Oh, this person is called Master, so he must have great realization; he may even be enlightened," and so on. We project many different ideas about "teacher" onto the human personality who holds that title. And because we feel that such masters possess knowledge beyond our own, they become, in our mind, a little bit like gods. Being in their presence becomes intimidating, and we feel the need to please, obey, or compliment them. This is not an expression of genuine respect, however, and it's not the original intention of the Buddha, who spoke of the spiritual *friend*—not a master or disciplinarian. Sometimes you hear a student say, "If I do such and such, my teacher will get upset." Are you sure? Think about it. Beyond your imagination, what might happen? Do you really know this person well enough to predict his or her thoughts and emotions? In any case, the point of the spiritual path is not to please any single person; it's to become free of ignorance, to become fully who we are. So appeasement is the wrong concept. Instead we should examine ourselves and be aware of our motivations. Then we can say, "Yes, this is a proper course of action," or "No, if I do such and such, then I'm going to screw up my spiritual journey and destroy my vision of freedom." That's a saner way to relate with such thoughts.

We must pay attention to our use of language and how it impacts our mind. The words that we in the West are now adapting from other languages are purely our own choice. We have chosen words like *teacher, master,* and *guru* as titles for the people to whom we go for spiritual training and counsel. But the original Buddhist term is *spiritual friend.*

An authentic spiritual friend should have two main qualities. The first is to be learned, to have both vast knowledge of the Buddhist teachings and profound insight into their meaning. The second is to hold correct ethical discipline, which is the basis for maintaining all the trainings of the Buddhist path. These are what we should look for when seeking a teacher, or an ally, on our path. Since we're looking for just these two qualities, it should be very easy to find someone like this, right? It just takes a few years, or lifetimes, to develop these qualities. If we're fortunate enough to meet such a true friend, he or she can become a great source of inspiration and guidance for us. And the point at which we're ready for such a relationship seems to signal the time when we're becoming more serious about our path.

This kind of friendship can make all the difference in our spiritual journey. Our teacher may be the first person toward whom we really open our heart, the first one with whom we're willing to be totally truthful. It's a significant relationship we're making with another human being. It can become our entrance to a larger world, our introduction to what it means to truly see and embrace all forms and dimensions of humanity, including our own. Because of its significance, we need to understand this relationship and make it a real one.

Teacher as CEO

The spiritual friend is a person with whom you can have a relationship as a friend rather than as an authority figure, boss, or CEO of your organization. You can discuss your practice and share your experiences on the path with your friend, and he or she can give you practical advice, guidance, and support for your journey. We need to understand this, because frankly we're missing this element today in many of our Tibetan Buddhist organizations. Especially in the West, we need to go back to the original root meaning of "spiritual friend" and bring about that quality.

If we look at the development of many of our Buddhist organizations in the West, we can see that they're structured and function much like corporations. In some sense, this model offers many advantages in terms of efficiency, and it's even necessary in terms of relating to legal and financial regulations. The days of mom-and-pop Buddhism are mostly behind us. In many cases, this means that the head, or president, of the organization will be the teacher. In earlier times, the main teacher would be the abbot of the monastery, a parallel situation. So in addition to spiritual instruction, there is business to be taken care of, projects to be managed, conference calls to convene, directors to be appointed, and volunteers to be managed. It's fertile ground for the practice of mindfulness and compassion, to be sure, but this approach also has pitfalls that we need to avoid.

Is your teacher now your boss, who sets deadlines for turning out reports and budgets, or is your teacher now an employee of the organization, who must generate revenue through programs, embark on goodwill tours, and answer to the board of directors? If we regard our spiritual friend as some kind of chief executive officer, then all we need to do is make sure he or she is doing that job. Otherwise, if the organization is losing money or market share, or we're not getting enlightened, then we can fire him or her, like booting a CEO out of an underperforming company. In this scenario, the pedestal has become an executive chair, and all conversations become status reports or negotiations. Where is the quality of friendship in all this?

Friends don't always talk about business or problems. There's a need for some sense of spaciousness, openness, and relaxation. When you go out for coffee with a friend, you don't immediately start negotiating a contract or trying to confirm a schedule. You just go out for coffee and enjoy the companionship. Or when you go out to a bar, you just enjoy your drink with your friend. When it's time to talk business, certainly you must do that, but there's a beginning and end to it. When the meeting is over, you let it go. When it's time to discuss your practice and personal life, you know you'll have the full attention and compassionate concern of your friend, but when that discussion is over, you let that go as well.

If you can't let go and keep pushing your business or personal agenda on your friend 24/7, then that's a good way of losing your friend. There's no sense of real closeness; it's just contracts, deals, and "woe is me." In a sane relationship with a friend, you don't talk just about your needs and troubles all the time. That kind of self-centered approach backfires on you. Instead of gaining support and good advice, your friend gets frustrated with you and begins to avoid you. If you call your friend's cell phone, no answer; home phone, no answer; e-mail, no answer.

The Two-Way Street

It's necessary for us to see what friendship means at every level of the relationship. Spiritual life and mundane life are not antithetical. Teacher and friend are not worlds apart. There is no teacher who isn't a human being, who doesn't have needs, who never feels pleasure and pain. This has been true from the Buddha's time to the present. Therefore, as friends, we must help each other as sincerely as we can. When your friend is in need, then you're there, doing your job as a friend, helping that person in whatever way you can. Friendship doesn't flow in just one direction; it's a two-way street. The well-being of both people is involved.

This outlook toward our teacher as friend should come from the heart and be uncontrived. It's not just a thought that we're trying to impose. If we relate to each other as friends, then we can bring down the barriers between us. No gap is necessary. Then the power of the spiritual friend to help us give rise to awakened heart can function freely. There's a benefit to the relationship for the student, because the spiritual friend can be relied on to nurture our understanding and positive qualities. He or she will also be honest with us by pointing out our blind spots and self-deceptions. In short, the spiritual friend can be said to be the most fundamental cause for the awakening of our potential, in the sense that he or she guides us on the path, explains the teachings and practices, and is a model for us of someone who is prepared to be totally truthful and is fearlessly willing to work with the confusion of others.

Whether you see your friend every day or once in a blue moon, that contact can be so intimate and striking that it penetrates right to the heart. Once you've opened the door and invited this unusual character in, there may be a moment of panic when you see all your preconceptions flying out the window. Yet there you are, feeling a little naked, a little suspicious, a little intoxicated. Is this person the perfect buddha you imagined—or a crazy person? Or, worst case scenario, is your friend simply ordinary—nothing special at all? We have all kinds of thoughts, which isn't particularly a problem. Our friend may even fuel our doubts and suspicions until we get beyond the frenzy of thoughts to something we recognize as real or true. Finding out who our friend is, it turns out, is a way to find out who we are. Are we a buddha, crazy, or ordinary? Our friend simply mirrors our hopes and fears without distortion until we come to recognize our own face, our own heart.

Showing Respect

How should you act in the presence of such a spiritual friend? You might follow the example of others: stand up, sit down, bow, prostrate, speak, or remain silent when others do. That's one way to learn the traditional protocols taught for showing respect to teachers and the teachings. Such gestures are appropriate at times, primarily if you're in a shrine hall, where images of buddhas and Buddhist texts are displayed and you're gathered with your community of fellow practitioners. Then you might feel that you're within a sacred environment together, and so placing your hands at your heart, you bow your head. You don't need a manual for that. But if you meet your teacher in public (at a Starbucks, for example), a hello or a handshake is sufficient, unless you wish to show your respect for the establishment and its patrons and your faith in the basic goodness of its coffee and croissants.

Your conduct in the presence of your spiritual friend doesn't have to be formal or complicated. You can push yourself to learn all the proper forms of respect, but all your bows and prostrations will be nothing but empty gestures, devoid of meaning, if there's no genuine feeling behind them. If you naturally feel a sense of appreciation, affection, and trust toward your friend, then respect is something that comes automatically. You don't have to build up your respect intentionally or worry about sticking to all the traditional forms. Your respect will be naturally evident in your presence and all your actions. Whether you're standing up straight or offering a simple bow, nothing will be missing. But if you don't feel a sense of trust or appreciation naturally, then you may need the etiquette manuals, the idiot's guides to everything. On the other hand, you can just relax and be who you are and see what happens.

The Buddha taught that having a spiritual friend will help you on your journey to liberation. It changes your trip and makes it more powerful and vivid. It also makes it more fun. You're together on the road to freedom. Whether the territory you're passing through seems familiar or strange and new, you're not finding your way alone; you have a guide and companion you can rely on. The further you go, the more awake you feel. The more awake you are, the more you feel that you're finally becoming your true self. Once you hit that spot, there's no turning back. Going beyond self, you discover the overwhelming power of selfless love and compassion. Beauty is everywhere because mind is beautiful. That's what we call the awakened heart.

what's in your mouth

THERE IS A Tibetan saying: "What's in your mouth is also in your hand." It describes people who are not just talk; they put their words into action. In America, we say that people like this "walk the talk" or "practice what they preach."

We actively bring the practice of compassion and the attitude of altruism into our life in two ways. The first is through developing a strong and clear intention to do so, which is like thinking something through for a long time and then coming to a conclusion. What we're thinking about in this case is, how seriously and how far are we going to take this? It's a big question. If we decide to commit to it, to do it, then we make that promise a part of our being; we own it. That's the first step. The second step is that we start to do whatever it takes to live up to that aspiration, which otherwise remains just words. What do we need to do? We need to wake up so we can help others to wake up as well. It's difficult for someone who's asleep to rouse someone else from sleep, even if the other person is in the same room having a terrible nightmare.

The shift from aspiration to action takes place in our day-to-day activities. We start to reverse some of our egocentric habits and replace them with words and actions that benefit others. These can be small things, but you have to start somewhere. You can't just wait until your good intentions transform themselves into positive actions. If you're content with the belief that "someday I'll be really generous and disciplined and become helpful to others," that's magical thinking. Instead of dreaming of that day, you can put your words into practice by taking one step at a time but taking that step repeatedly. As you change your thinking, your actions will change, and as you change your actions, your thinking will begin to change, and so on.

However, don't take on anything that's too challenging or ambitious. Try something you know you can do and go slowly. Ironically, it's our own sense of inspiration that sometimes trips us up. If you overreach and fail, then what? You risk discouragement and the collapse of your whole vision. You might feel that such a noble heart is too much for an ordinary person. Then you're liable to apply that logic to the whole path and think, "Oh no, this isn't for me," when, in fact, your only problem was being unskillful in some of your actions.

Don't Eat Anything Bigger than Your Head

One day, I was with some friends in a restaurant in Asia, and one hungry lama ordered a large burger. He knew it was going to be big, but when it arrived at the table, it turned out to be extraordinarily big. It was huge. I've never seen anything like it. At that moment, a Westerner walked by and said to the lama, "Don't eat anything that's bigger than your head!" In the same way, don't attempt anything on the spiritual path that's too much for you to handle.

You can start your practice of compassion with your family and circle of friends, extend that to friends of friends, and then gradually move on to everyone you meet. Of course, you should maintain your sense of larger vision, but in actual practice, it has to be one-on-one. A single act of generosity, for example, won't eradicate global poverty. If you have five dollars, you can't give it to everyone in the world. But if there's one guy in front of you who really needs those five dollars, you can give them to him. They can buy a bowl of soup and eliminate one person's hunger and feeling of desperation—for a while, at least. That's an act of generosity, and it's how you can practice in a way that's both personal and practical.

Transcendent Action

The Buddha was known for giving teachings that harmonized with the attitudes, dispositions, and interests of the people who gathered to hear him. He matched his instruction to the capabilities of his audience. We can take the Buddha's teaching style as an example as we try to guide ourselves in how to practice compassion. We can concentrate on things that match our own interests, abilities, and resources.

Practicing compassion is very ordinary in some sense. We're simply cultivating the qualities recognized by most societies as being good and signs of a moral character. However, what we're doing here is a bit different, because we're joining "good works" with the view of twofold selflessness. Earlier, when we worked with the ten positive actions, we were still trying to understand our own selflessness. But now we approach what we're doing with the outlook of awakened heart. I say *outlook* because it's something we're working toward.

By practicing with this outlook, you start to change your ordinary perception of yourself and others. You start to feel less like you're the center of the universe. You go beyond self, letting down your shield of defense. When you reach out to someone, you are totally in the open. You can be genuinely who you are without any agenda. That means you don't look at the other person as an extension of your trip or as part of your big-deal project of compassion. The other person is label free. Therefore, you have to deal with that person as who he or she really is.

It's important to remember that you're not creating selflessness here. You're not taking a solid self and performing an alchemical feat of changing it into emptiness. You and I are naturally selfless right now, and by developing the view of selflessness, you're only learning to act in accordance with your real nature. When you can do that pretty well, then you recognize that selflessness is who you really are. It's not a new you, a new other, or a new world. It's simply an open world without all the unnecessary fixations we usually impose on it. It's naturally a world of freedom with unlimited resources of loving-kindness.

When you apply the view of awakened heart to the practice of any compassionate action, that practice, that action becomes pure. This means that it's free of "you" clinging to it and making it all about you. In more traditional, philosophical terms, I'd say that it's free from fixation. First, however, you have to see your attachments and fixations clearly. Seeing an attachment clearly means that you see not only the attachment itself but also its momentary quality. It's not one continuous, solid thing. It's just moments that add up, if you let them. When you remember that, you can relax and release your clinging. That's what makes it possible to truly give, to truly be kind, to truly be a best friend. The view of awakened heart fits with all your practices. It's what makes an ordinary action a transcendent, or selfless, one.

The method we use to transform ordinary actions into transcendent ones—which is to say, the means we use to cultivate awakened heart—focuses on six activities and the mind states that accompany them. We've met some of them before, but we're working with all six in a particular way here. They are generosity, discipline, patience, diligence, meditation, and higher knowledge. When we commit to practicing these activities with the view of awakened heart, we go beyond just thinking about stepping out of the DMZ; we actually do it. This is where we see the value of our preparations and test our skills under the fire of real anger, real jealousy, real desire, and real pride. By including others in our practice, the situation is amplified, because we're not dealing with our own neurosis alone but also with the neuroses coming at us from others.

So this becomes a true test of how serious we are and how far we're willing to go. Can we stick to our altruistic motivation when we're being attacked by someone we intended to help? When we feel vulnerable and exposed to the judgments of others, do we revert to a strategy of pre-emptive strikes? It's not one big battle we're facing that will decide everything; it's the most simple and commonplace encounters in our daily life that test our courage and willingness to open our heart fearlessly. There's always the possibility of trusting our rebel buddha mind to carry us beyond our ordinary instincts and hesitation. Sometimes we'll succeed and sometimes we'll fail, but as long as we keep coming back to our original intention, that's the essence of transcendent practice.

Transcendent Generosity

Ordinarily, when you give something to someone, there's a strong sense of self-consciousness involved in the whole event. You're aware of yourself as the giver, as well as your act of giving and the experience of the person who is getting your gift. There are a lot of concepts and attachments involved in the simple act of giving a present. There's a sense of wanting to be recognized as the giver: "This is mine, and now I'm giving it to you." However, when you apply the view of awakened heart to this process, generosity becomes a practice of letting go of all those concepts. That makes it possible to truly give, to perform an act of authentic generosity, which is selfless.

The point is not to be judgmental of your own actions or those of others. When you give, you just give. You don't have to ask, "Am I giving properly? Am I feeling the right feelings? Am I being a good person?" All of these "Am I's" become a problem. The key to generosity in its transcendent sense is to give without reservation, without any sort of self-consciousness or worry. As long as you second-guess yourself or are apprehensive about the reactions and opinions of others, your generosity is not pure. It's the conventional mind of hope and fear clothed in propriety. On the other hand, if somebody to whom you have given a gift becomes judgmental and fills his or her head with all kinds of negative thoughts about your gift, that's not your problem. Your problem is just giving, and as long as you've given with an open, selfless heart, then your act of generosity has been completed and is pure.

Transcendent generosity is simply a willingness to be open and do whatever is necessary in the moment, without any philosophical or religious rationale. Seeing someone in need, you're willing to share your wealth, your happiness, or your wisdom, and you're also willing to share in the pain of others. Yet when you give, you need to do so with the awareness that your gift will be both appropriate and helpful. It's not an act of generosity, for example, to give money to a wealthy person or alcohol to a child. You give what you can afford; you don't jeopardize your own health or well-being. At the same time, you can give what is precious to you, what is difficult to give because of your attachment to it.

Another kind of generosity is protection from fear. You do this when you provide physical or mental help to someone who's anxious or frightened. You may be able to ease his or her fear simply by being a calming presence and somebody to talk to. Or you may be able to provide a heated shelter in the winter to a person facing the terrors of the cold. Protecting a person or animal from harm in whatever way you can is the generosity of protection. You can also give protection from the fear of illness by providing medicine or from the fear of death by providing companionship, care, and spiritual counseling.

Such acts of openness can take place anywhere—in the middle of a rock concert, on a bus, or in a butcher shop. Who knows? You can apply this view of awakened heart to all your interactions with others, including yourself. Sometimes we talk to ourselves as if we were two people, "You're such an idiot! How could you be so stupid?" Then that "you" will benefit from the same kindness and openness as anyone else. Never forget to be generous to yourself while you're working so hard to extend yourself to others.

Transcendent Discipline

To practice discipline with the view of awakened heart, the key is to maintain a sense of mindfulness and awareness of your actions and the effects of those actions on others. It's important to pay special attention to anger and ill will and to stop them in their tracks. When you catch anger right away and hold it with your mindfulness, it's like rebel buddha intercepting a pass and preventing the other team—your angry thoughts and intentions—from scoring a touchdown. You don't allow your anger to reach the person you're mad at or to spill over to innocent bystanders. At the very least, you slow its momentum, which gives you a moment to relax your fixed mind and return to a state of openness. Instead of the fight you could have started, you can inject something different—a sense of humor or a kind word—into the situation. The shift in your outlook brings a sense of relief, not just to you, but to others as well. The practice of generosity is helpful here, because it inspires in you the desire to give happiness and protection from harm. When you refrain from anger, you're protecting others not just from your anger but also from becoming caught up in their own. In this way, you can practice generosity and discipline at the same time.

Transcendent Patience

We usually think of patience as forbearance. We're willing to endure a certain amount of frustration or pain in our life. When you practice patience with the outlook of awakened heart, however, it goes beyond the attitude of "keep a stiff upper lip" or "grin and bear it." Having patience can also mean that you don't react impulsively. Instead, you become curious about what's going on and take the time to see a situation clearly. If people are blaming you for their problems, then you take time to feel their frustration and see how they're suffering from their own disappointments and discouragement. Then instead of feeling resentment, you can offer understanding and encouragement. The difference is that your first thought is not how insulted you feel or how unfairly you're being treated. It's a voice of concern for the pain that is touching you and others equally and the thought of how to relieve it. When your patience is being tested, you need to recall your discipline of mindfulness to calm your impatience and help you see all the elements at play in what you're facing.

Another aspect of patience is not becoming discouraged when you try to help someone and your efforts aren't appreciated. You loan your brother-in-law a hundred dollars, and he complains that it's not two hundred. You give meditation instruction to a friend and are rebuffed the next week because he or she is still not enlightened. We need patience, too, in our meditation practice when we experience physical or psychological discomfort. It may be that your knee hurts or that you want to watch the new episode of your favorite TV show or check your computer for an "urgent" e-mail you're expecting. Or it may be a little more significant—the unease you might feel when you're facing the profound realities of selflessness. When you're at risk of losing your balance or inspiration, patience helps to maintain a steady, positive, and open mind.

Transcendent Diligence

Ordinarily we equate diligence with a lot of effort. On the one hand, there's a sense of physical or mental sweat. On the other, there's a sense of being a good, industrious boy or girl—we're working hard toward a goal and not letting up. But being diligent on our spiritual path doesn't mean that we're meditating for hours, vacuuming the shrine room, and serving meals at a homeless shelter all in one day. Transcendent diligence means that we take whatever opportunities we have to practice, and we do those practices with a sense of appreciation and delight. In this sense, diligence is energy, the power that makes everything happen. It's like the wind, a driving force that keeps us moving along the path. Where does this energy come from? It comes from the enjoyment and satisfaction we experience as we get further into our path.

The primary obstacle to diligence is, of course, laziness—the absence of energy. One problem with laziness is that it takes up so much time. Think of how much time taking it easy or spacing out requires. The problem with activities like going to the beach or hanging out is not that they're negative; it's our attachment to them. I'm sure more people go to the "beach" that's a state of mind than to all the resorts in Mexico. Laziness shows up in other ways too. We can be attached to bad ideas or bad friends, or we can tell ourselves that we don't have what it takes to be on this path. We can also get stuck in laziness by just remaining very busy all the time and never making time for our practice. So in the beginning, some ordinary exertion is required.

Yet when we break through our habits just a little, we begin to feel this rising breeze of delight. As it grows stronger, we become so inspired that no matter what happens, we never lose our sense of appreciation or enthusiasm for our path. Then whatever we do becomes as effortless as sailing on the open sea. The work of getting away from the shore and catching the wind has already been done. All that's left to do is just to keep our hand on the tiller.

Transcendent Meditation

The practice of meditation here is not much different from our earlier practices of calm abiding and clear seeing, which steadily increase the power of our concentration and the sharpness of our intellect. Since we've already discussed these methods in some detail, it's not necessary to describe them again. However, when you bring the outlook of awakened heart to your practice of meditation, the power of your practice intensifies.

When you look at your mind now, it's not like you're just hanging out with a new friend in a café, drinking chamomile tea and listening to each other's stories. You've done that. You've already made friends with your mind, and now you're ready to see beyond the level of thoughts and emotions to the mind's true nature.

When you reach this point, you can ask your spiritual friend for special meditation instructions on how to look directly at your mind. It's like going to the barista at the café and saying you're ready for something a little stronger, a grande mocha or macchiato, something that will really wake you up. Like the boost you get from an espresso, the instructions you get from your spiritual friend energize and wake up your meditation practice. You begin to see what you have never seen before—the transparent, radiant awareness that is mind's true nature. When you recognize your own awareness at this level of meditation, it's like waking up from a dream. Before, you were fooled by the dream appearances created by your customary thoughts. As these begin to dissolve, you realize, "Oh, that was just a dream. Now I'm awake."

The practice of meditation, in this sense, is a way to step further into the space of openness and joy that you've started to discover. It's how you wake up to the brilliant clarity and panoramic awareness of the experience of emptiness. Eventually, you reach a point where you can click into a state of wakefulness anywhere or anytime. You don't have to be sitting up straight on a cushion. You could be working at your computer, picking up your kids from school, or sitting at the bedside of a sick friend. At that point, except for mindfulness, all you need to bring to any situation is the thought of compassion.

Transcendent Knowledge

Transcendent knowledge is not so much a practice as a result of all our previous practices. What we come to know at this point is the reality of twofold selflessness, or emptiness. When this realization dawns, it comes without concepts or words. It's something we know directly, in a personal way. At first there are glimpses of emptiness, then experiences that come and go; finally we get the full experience. We understand what is meant by nowness, openness, and all the rest. It's the moment that any uneasiness or fear we had about selflessness, or emptiness, is put to rest. It's an experience of lightheartedness and freedom, joy and boundless love. It is absolute—absolutely there, absolutely clear, absolutely complete. This more panoramic experience of emptiness is called "emptiness with a heart of compassion." The five previous transcendent practices are what prepare us to realize emptiness. Through them, we learn to let go of fixation and develop a strong heart of compassion. But it's the practice of meditation that is most influential. It's the most direct cause of the superior seeing that leads to this insight. It's the space in which understanding takes place without thought or words.

When we reach the level of realization, there's no space left for ego or self-centered views and actions. We are entirely selfless, yet at the same time, our whole being is compassion. We could look at it from one side or the other, emptiness or compassion, and it would make little difference. Is water fluid or wet? Is fire bright or hot? Like a mute person tasting sugar for the first time, we're full of knowing that is inexpressible through words or signs. When we reach this state, that is ultimate experience, and it's time to wake up.

Are We There Yet?

This is a good time to ask, "What happens to our spiritual journey when we're doing well, when we're more or less happy and satisfied with our life?" We've pulled ourselves up and out of the depths of our suffering. Our minds are well trained and steady. We're free from the withering heat of our emotions. We've practiced all the virtues, and our hearts are open. We feel we're in the clear. We're confident that if we just keep going straight ahead, we'll arrive at our destination. Even so, there's no particular hurry anymore, because we are now enjoying the ride so much.

There's an old English proverb: "There's many a slip twixt the cup and the lip." That means that even though we're holding the cup in our hand, something could happen before we drink the wine. We think,

"I'm going to enjoy drinking this delicious wine," and then we get distracted, trip over ourselves, and it's all gone. So even though we're close, we're not there yet.

Like the heroes and heroines of stories and like Buddha himself, the greatest tests often come toward the end of our journey. What do they test? Our genuineness. Are we who we think we are? If not, misunderstanding and attachment can creep back in, in one form or another. When that happens, we lose our vision of emptiness and create more concepts. Then we simply end up with another version of self, one that's more refined and harder to see. We can be fooled because we have such a strong concept of emptiness and habit of labeling everything as self-less. But even a correct concept or intellectual understanding is not the same as realization. In fact, it's the accomplishments we do have that can become the basis of a spiritual ego that manifests as pride and clinging to our "good" self.

On our good days, we may have excellent experiences of emptiness. We feel joyful, with a sense of meaning and purpose. On our bad days, emptiness sucks. We have all kinds of doubts and think, "This is bullshit. What's my teacher talking about? Emptiness, what's so empty about it? It's so real it hurts." Those kinds of fluctuation in our experience are what we call unstable experiences. In some sense, they're not trustworthy. If we use them properly, however, they contribute to our understanding and point us in the right direction. A breakthrough or positive experience can be inspirational and important for our development, but there are many stories about how great meditators were fooled by early signs of enlightenment that they took to be the real thing.

Once there was a very good meditator in Tibet. He was practicing emptiness meditation in a cave. At one point, he rested his hand on the rocky floor of the cave, and at the end of his session, he realized his hand had made an imprint in the rock. This is a famous sign in Tibet for realization, and he was impressed by his own achievement. He thought, "Oh, I've realized emptiness now." Then he thought, "If I could do this in front of my students, it would be even better. They would be amazed!" So the next time he gathered his students together, they meditated in the cave for a while. At the end of their session, with the intention of making an imprint, he slapped his hand on the rock quite hard, and when he lifted it, there was nothing but a pink palm.

It's possible to have experiences that are like the signs of realization but are just temporary. They're good to have, but if we grow attached to them and see them as the real thing, then we may get fooled like many meditators in the past. Therefore, we first develop the experience of emptiness; then, without getting attached to it, we can gradually stabilize it and bring it to full realization. Attachment to experiences prevents us from moving on. So it's really up to us whether we want to get stuck with one little experience of feeling great or move on to full awakening. As far as the path is concerned, there's always a need to go beyond the sparks that ignite before an experience starts to blaze. It's like trying to start a fire without matches and having to use something else, like rocks. At first when you strike the rocks together, you get a lot of sparks. If you become fascinated by the sparks, you might just keep striking the rocks, saying, "Wow! Look at that!" The sparks are beautiful, of course, but you'll never get your tea boiled if you stay at the level of "Wow!" In the same way, if you become fascinated by flashes of insight and glimpses of emptiness, then realization never ignites. There's no sense of deepening your experiences, and the fire never comes.

Even the knowledge we do have can become the cause of clinging again when we become proud of it. "Look at everything I know—so much more than the average Joe." We get a little puffed up and self-important. It's hard to let go because it feels good, and it's not really doing anyone any harm, right? We all have moments of ordinary pride on our path, and we should be proud of our accomplishments. As long as you're willing to let go of your pride, you can use your accomplishments as inspiration to go further. But if you don't let go, then ego starts building its spiritual house again, adding a second story, a rec room, and a swimming pool, creating a little paradise you won't want to leave.

One way to avoid getting stuck is not to keep talking about your experiences—either to yourself or others. It's helpful to discuss them with your spiritual friend or share them with a few trusted fellow meditators once, maybe twice, but not more. The most common way of getting stuck is by constantly circling back to them in your thought processes. So it's necessary to exert yourself at a certain point if you want to go further, if you're ready not only to practice good deeds but also to give rise to this thing called emptiness with a heart of compassion.

Attachment to virtue is an equally powerful agent of clinging. When our mind is so deeply rooted in a concept of virtue, letting go of our identity as a "good person" can be problematic. Our whole journey until now has brought us to the point of being good—in fact, exceptionally good. In this world of confusion and conflict, we've become professional positive thinkers and problem solvers with no thought of reward or recognition for ourselves. The danger here is that we can become so attached to our practice of virtue that it becomes who we think we are. When our compassion strays from its connection to emptiness, we end up with another solid, dualistic identity, and our virtue becomes conventional goodness. This kind of virtue can still produce some good in the world, but it has limits. The goal of this path is limitless compassion, a morality that sees beyond labels.

Another trap is becoming complacent. We can become too cozy with our neurosis. We're so familiar with it that the problems it poses don't seem so bad. We end up being too lazy to get out of our comfortable, secure spot to deal with our basic clinging and dualistic values. The idea of a journey that will take us all the way to liberation sounds good. It's a very romantic idea. We can read about the lives of historical figures like the great Indian yogi Tilopa and his student Naropa and say, "Wow, that's beautiful. I wish I had a teacher like that." That's easy to say when you're on your nice futon bed piled with comfortable pillows, with a reading light that you can adjust so that the light falls perfectly on the page, and next to the lamp there's a cold beer. People often tell me how inspiring these traditional stories are. Strangely enough, many of them describe how students endured almost unbearable physical hardships and what we might today call psychological torture at the hands of their teachers. Still, we wish we were following one of these enlightened figures, who we imagine could wake us up just by snapping their fingers. But what we're really saying is that we wish we could wake up just by reading about it. We don't really want to undertake the hard work or psychological pressures that someone like Naropa went through for the sake of his freedom.

At some point, we really need to leap from our comfortable spot and go beyond imagining this road to freedom to actually traveling it. It's a growing-up process. When we were kids, it was natural to be fanciful. Kids spend a lot of time imagining adventures until they can start living them; they might fantasize about building robots or flying to Mars. But in order for our path to actually work, we need to stop clinging to our fantasy of the spiritual journey and face its reality.

As the Buddha taught, we meet self-clinging in the beginning, in the middle, and at the end of our path. Once we've transformed everything else, the final thing that remains before we "click" into the state of total freedom is a subtle level of clinging. As long as we're holding on here, we can't be there, in the actual state of selflessness. In my experience, there seems to be a need for some kind of push at this point.

turning up the heat

THE BASIC FOCUS of our journey at this point is transcending the last traces of our self-clinging. That clinging may be so subtle that it's barely discernable to us. Yet its effect is quite powerful. We're still bound to our identity and can't figure out how to get past this final hang-up. It's like the fine line that marks the border between two countries. We are on one side, loyal citizens of our country and culture of concepts. On the other side is a foreign land, a country of no culture and no concepts. From the tales we've heard, it's a mysterious place whose secrets are revealed only to those who actually enter it. Shall we stay or go? It's so close that we could take one step and be there, but we can't quite do it. What's holding us back?

For all the questioning we've done and all the knowledge we've gained from it, we find that we still have one final question, one final doubt. We simply don't know and can't know what it really means to let go of clinging to this "self" of ours until we actually do it. We want to take that leap of faith, but we want to do a test run first with a bungee cord or parachute. Or we want someone to hold our hand and leap with us. Like the fairy tale children, Hansel and Gretel, we want to leave a trail of bread crumbs so we can find our way back home to our familiar sense of self, if we don't like it out there in the selfless, open world.

When we set out on the road to that discovery, it's like taking a journey back to mind's original state. At first, we think that we're going somewhere, that freedom is up ahead, but actually our trip is simply a process that brings us back to our starting point—where we were before we left home to wander in the forest of our conceptualizations. Even though we've been gone from our home so long that we can't remember what it looks like, it's where our heart is and where we long to be.

What we need at this point is for somebody to turn up the psychological heat until our mental fixations have dissolved enough for us to take that leap. The best person to do this is our spiritual friend, whom we already know and trust. It's our good friend who can help us leap from our comfortable spot, who can help us let go of our subtle clinging and pride in our identity—whatever that identity is at this point. Between us and our freedom, there remains just a thin veil of ignorance that still has the power of a brick wall to keep us imprisoned in the state of duality. Beyond that wall is open space that is free of all reference points of impure-pure, confused-awake, or jerk-nice guy or gal. If we want this kind of help getting to the other side, it's up to us to go to our friend and ask for it.

Spiritual Friend as Special Agent

In the Tibetan Buddhist tradition, once a student has a good foundation of practice, it's possible to seek a teacher-student relationship that goes further than friendship alone. In this relationship, the teacher becomes a more formidable agent in the student's process of awakening. However, such a relationship must be instigated by the student. We must approach our spiritual friend and ask him or her to take a stronger hand in our awakening process. In essence, we're saying, "I know that I have everything I need to reach my destination on my own, but I'm requesting your help to get there faster. Please help me wake up in whatever way you think will work. If I don't leap myself, then you have my permission to pull the ground out from under me."

If our spiritual friend agrees, then the relationship changes. In the new relationship, the teacher is in the driver's seat, using his or her own map, which may not look quite like ours. Now, the teacher is no longer just our emotional support, friendly counselor, and instructor. Something new is added. He or she may appear in one moment as our buddy and in the next as our boss. Our teacher may praise us today and ignore or scold us tomorrow. Furthermore, when our teacher gives us an instruction about our spiritual practice now, we don't hear it as a suggestion; we hear it as a clear direction to be followed. We don't say, "No, I have a better idea." We trust that our teacher sees what's best for us in a spiritual sense; we're not asking him or her what to do about our taxes, how to vote in the next election, or how to repair our car. We have to take care of our own life.

At the same time that we're working with these instructions, we may begin to see qualities in our teacher we have never seen before. Our spiritual friend may suddenly appear to be unpredictable, unreasonable, or even bad-tempered, which can be a little bit scary. We don't always know where we stand in this new relationship. Yet we start to notice a shift taking place within our psyche. There is suddenly more energy available to us—a heightened sense of passion and joy, anger and clarity, and so on. Emotional flare-ups begin to illuminate, rather than obscure, our vision. This is somewhat new territory for us. We find we're being seduced out of our purely conceptual existence into a freer and rawer reality.

Entering into this kind of relationship is not a step to be taken lightly. Such a course of action is not suitable for every student or every teacher. Our goal of full awakening can, without doubt, be accomplished through the methods laid out previously. Our destination—freedom— is no different, whether we maintain our original relationship with our spiritual friend or enter into this new relationship. It's simply an option that agrees well with some but not with others. The advantages are that our journey may be much quicker, and we may be introduced by our spiritual friend to further methods for bringing about the recognition of the nature of mind. The disadvantage is that the journey is more rugged and psychologically challenging; whatever it is that we cling to will be made vividly apparent by our friend through direct or indirect means. It goes without saying that there needs to be a strong sense of respect and trust between teacher and student, but there also needs to be a sense of chemistry—a sense of heat and interest, rapport and spark.

WHOM DO YOU TRUST? SURRENDERING TO THE HIGHER POWER OF THE MIND

In our Western democratic cultures, such a relationship is likely to be questioned, and rightly so. We don't want to become a member of a cult with a charismatic leader or give up our own good sense and judgment. If we lose those things, there is no journey to personal freedom. So we must examine the situation carefully.

Although we live with the illusion that we're freethinkers and make our own decisions, we give away our independence of thought quite often. In fact, there are so many "authorities" in our life, it's difficult to sort them all out. Everyone is telling us what to think and do: Is abortion okay or not? Should we vote for gay marriage? Do we want more guns or none at all? Should smoking be banned? Should murderers be executed or jailed for life? Whom do you look to when you're trying to come up with "your own" answers? Whom do you trust on the big questions? Your favorite celebrity, your political party, the president, the pope?

Moreover, our thinking about things like power and authority is not always consistent. While, on the one hand, we rail against a government takeover, on the other hand, we spend much of our life following trends set by unknown powerbrokers that do nothing for us but empty our pockets. Our relationship with our spiritual friend is intended to do something for us; the only reason it exists is to help us reclaim our genuine independence. It's a relationship based on knowledge and trust, which is the most powerful kind of relationship we can have. That's why businesses are always saying things like, "You can trust us."

Perhaps the closest thing in Western culture to this kind of teacher-student relationship is found in the Twelve-Step program of Alcoholics Anonymous (A.A.). A.A. and similar programs provide valuable support for recovery from debilitating addictions, and an essential element of recovery involves a process of spiritual awakening, or "surrender," in which people recognize that they can let go of trying to deal with their problem alone. They can surrender their personal struggle to a higher power, whatever they conceive that to be. Many people have reported that the moment they made that decision was the moment they experienced their first sense of healing, the beginning of their journey back to physical, emotional, and spiritual health.

From the Buddhist perspective, self-clinging is an addiction that we're often powerless to stop on our own, regardless of the suffering it brings to us or others. So just as we would seek support for recovery from a substance dependency from a group like A.A., we can seek support for recovery from self-clinging from the teachings of the Buddha and, specifically, from our own teacher. What we surrender to, our higher power, is the awakened nature of mind itself, which is intrinsically healthy and compassionate. In this way, we trust in the healing power of mind, and it is the teacher who guides us to make this connection during the period in which we can't be reliable guides for ourselves. Spiritual awakening is the key to full recovery, just as in the Twelve Steps, as described here:

> Spiritual awakenings are often described as just that, awakenings. They represent a coming to conscious awareness of ourselves as we really are, an awareness of a power greater than ourselves, which may be outside ourselves, or deep within ourselves, or both. Where there was darkness, now there is light. We can see things more realistically. Indeed we can see things we never saw before. Most people experience a sense of letting go. But in addition, many of us, especially women, report a gaining of power, a coming to our true selves after surrendering. There is a sense of grounding of ourselves in a power we didn't know before.[1]

When we start to let go of ego-clinging, the healing power of this "higher mind" can come through. On the Buddhist path, we're not surrendering to our teacher; we're surrendering our confused self to our true self. It's a process of awakening to who we truly are. It's our teacher who models the awakened state for us, and it's our teacher who knows and can subvert all the old tricks of an ego addict. Therefore, when we enter this relationship, we say, "I trust you to see me through this and am willing to accept your absolute honesty and tough love until I've recovered from my addiction."

Essentially, our spiritual friend has our permission to turn up the heat, to push our buttons, to add fuel to our fire of wisdom so that it blazes more intensely and burns up our self-clinging. We trust our teacher to do this and also to make sure that the fire doesn't get out of control and become destructive. In this sense, it's like a controlled burn in a forest to make it more healthy and productive.

LINEAGE

Although each tradition is different, there are criteria that clearly state the qualifications both teacher and student must meet in order to engage in such a relationship. These guidelines are meant to ensure that the relationship will be beneficial on both sides. For example, the teacher must hold a genuine lineage of the Buddha, be deeply learned, and possess both great realization and compassion. The student must be spiritually mature and committed to this course. When these conditions exist, then a spiritually accomplished teacher and a spiritually mature student can enter into a relationship that can bring about a rapid transformation of neurosis into its original state of wisdom.

What is lineage? In one sense, it refers to the succession of people who, from the time of the Buddha, received, accomplished, and then passed on the wisdom that leads to the awakened state. In another sense, lineage is wisdom itself, the content of what is passed on from teacher to student, generation after generation. We could also say it's the process of transmission, the ongoing communication of wisdom from accomplished people to their spiritual offspring and the nurturing of that wisdom until those children are mature, independent, and strong enough to pass it on to others. In this sense, the historical figures in the Buddhist tradition are our ancestors, the forebears of our realization. Because they passed on methods for awakening, we're able to connect with the same methods today. So we can think of lineage as our family tree.

the good shepherd and the outlaw

WHEN WE'RE GETTING ready to wake up, our journey becomes very, very basic. No matter who we are in the eyes of the world, we're just trying to leave this neurotic life behind and become more sane and compassionate people. We're trying to be virtuous, good shepherds, like Samuel Jackson's character at the end of the movie *Pulp Fiction*. In one of the final scenes, he's sitting in a restaurant holding a gun with his finger on the trigger, trying not to shoot the crazy people in front of him. He's hoping that he can just walk away without killing anyone. He's an outlaw, a bad guy, praying for the will or grace from above to become a good man firmly on the side of the angels.

That moment, where life and death or heaven and hell seem to hang in the balance, is the kind of intensified experience that offers the possibility of a different outcome altogether: freedom from all concepts on the spot. However, it has nothing to do with weapons. It has to do with our emotions, which, in their heightened state, can have the power and force of a loaded gun. To be clear, I'm not saying it's okay to fool around with guns or emotions, because that's how people get hurt. I'm saying that emotions are much more powerful in bringing about the experience of awakening than we think. If we can be fully present in the space of any emotion in its naked, raw state without conceptualizing it, then we stand a chance of transcending our dualistic mind right then and there. If, however, we fall back into mundane thoughts of good and bad, right and wrong, then we fall back into a conventional mind-set that says we're either saints or sinners—good shepherds or outlaws. We're still living in a conceptual, divided world, where one side is always in opposition to the other. We're still attaching labels to naked reality.

At this point in our journey, our perspective shifts. We begin to see that the very experience of our emotions is the experience of wakefulness. We no longer regard our emotions simply as "bad energy" or see them as just a form of potential. We usually think of anger, for example, as negative. Ordinarily, our impulse would be either to cut through it and get rid of it or to transform its intense energy into good qualities like clarity and patience. However, our project of recycling our disturbing emotions into positive mental states becomes redundant once we realize that our raw emotions and their pure essence are not, ultimately, any different. There's no need to peel away the outer layers of our emotions to find an inner essence called wakefulness, or enlightened wisdom.

Wisdom is not a treasure concealed inside our emotions. Openness and wakefulness are already present in that first flash of anger, passion, or jealousy. The distinction between mind and mind's true nature, or the emotions and their true nature, turns out to be valid only through the lens of thought. From their own side—their own perspective—no such distinctions can be made. Therefore, the direct experience of our unprocessed, raw emotions can generate a direct experience of wakefulness. These emotions are powerful agents in bringing about our freedom, if we can work with them properly.

This is admittedly a little tricky, which is why we rely so much on the guidance of our spiritual friend, who tells us now to trust our emotions even further. They are not only workable; they are the path and also its culmination. Their wakefulness is the wakefulness we seek. From this point of view, connecting with the experience of our original, primordial wakefulness is only possible when we can directly relate to and work with our raw emotions. While we may think of our messy, polluted mind as an embarrassment, our friend tells us not to look elsewhere to find a more presentable, respectable mind to make the basis of our spiritual journey.

That's the whole point and the beauty of this approach, as well as what makes it hard to accept. When our mind is deeply rooted in notions of virtue and sin, good and bad, and most of all, in the view of theism, then this kind of path is not possible for us. We have to find another, more gradual road to freedom. However, the teachings of the Buddha have many means for achieving realization, so we can choose what suits our temperament.

THE BRAVE FOOL

To leap into this kind of journey, we need the full cooperation of our rebel buddha mind. A certain degree of wildness or craziness is required—and where we may be hesitant or shy, rebel buddha is prepared to be bold and daring. There's a kind of heroism involved in being willing to step outside of our conventional thinking and challenge its ground rules. When we take that step, it can be a little difficult to tell if we're being courageous or just plain foolish. We have to be fearless, but that bravery must go hand in hand with an incisive intelligence and an open, questioning mind in order for this kind of venture to make sense.

In a way, it's like the stories we see in the movies. The hero has been a good boy (or girl) and lived a regular life. Then one day someone suddenly shows up, kills his parents, and kicks his butt. He has no idea why, but from that point on, he has to face extraordinary challenges. His family is dead, his money is gone, his reputation is ruined, and now his very life is at risk. Then he gets recruited by the CIA or the mob to do a nearly impossible job that will clear everything up, make him rich, and maybe bring him a little peace of mind in the process. Of course, it may kill him too, but that's a risk he has to take; he can't turn this opportunity down. He has no choice and nothing to lose. Have you seen this movie? By the end, our ordinary guy has faced so many dangers and struggles that he has become hopeless, fearless, and shameless. Consequently, he has also become free. When you have no hope, you have nothing to fear, nothing to be ashamed of, and nothing to lose. Then our hero is in a perfect position to see and act in ways that others can't. He can do whatever he has to do. If it's his job to become a thief, then he becomes the best thief. If it's to become an assassin, then he becomes the best hit man. And so the story goes, until he overcomes all obstacles, outwits all opponents, and ends up on top. That's the style of our journey here. We must navigate many levels of obstacles and land on our feet.

Meeting Neurosis Face-to-Face

The whole process we go through now is learning particular methods to work directly with our neurosis. When we talk about neurosis here, we're talking about our confused understanding of who we are and what the world is altogether. When we look at who we are, we see a picture of ourselves that is out of focus. As blurry as it is, we're attached to it: "Oh, look. There's a picture of me." We accept the picture as it is because it looks pretty normal to us. The other people in the photo and the trees in the background look about the same as we do. But we're not such good judges after all, because we have never seen a perfectly clear picture of ourselves.

Ordinarily, if we saw a photo of ourselves that was distorted or blurry, we'd know that's not what we really look like. We'd understand that the camera malfunctioned or the photographer goofed up. Our confused or neurotic self is like that blurry image. It's not a true or clear picture of who we are. What we're trying to do now is to get a clearer picture of ourselves and our world, one that is not distorted. The first step is to recognize that our picture is out of focus. The second step is to either clean up the master image or take a new picture.

So what's wrong with our picture—the portrait or image of ourselves that we have now? Our problem is that we don't see the true nature of our body, speech, and mind. Looking through the lens of confused mind, we see our body as something we possess and need to hold on to and protect, like a house with a sign out front saying, "Private property." We see our speech in terms of the labels and concepts we use to create and hang on to this world of duality. Our primary neurosis, however, is our fixation on mind or mental characteristics—the collection of individual traits that we identify as "me." And what constitutes the deepest aspect of our mental character is our system of values and principles. Who we are in this relative sense is, without a doubt, shaped by our culture and environmental conditioning, but also by our participation in that. We can't just blame our culture for who we are; we also participate. In the end, we're the ones who build up these characteristics into a solid identity. It is you and I who adopt what our culture feeds us; we own it and make it into our whole being.

We must look deeply at this area, because our values are a part of our cultural identity, our basic sense of self. This is where we'll find judgmental mind and also a sense of fear. Why? Because our values can function in both positive and negative ways. They can promote harmony, agreement, and understanding, or they can promote the opposite—conflict and aggression. When the values of two families are not in agreement, someone might get hurt. We need to discover anyplace where our mind has become closed to reason and questioning. When we don't know why we believe what we do, but we're still satisfied that we're right, that is blind faith—mind that's still in the dark. When we follow after our values with that kind of blind faith, we lose sight of their deeper meaning and power to guide and transform us. Then they become of no value.

All these apparent forms are what we take to be "me" and cling to so strongly. As the basis of our identity, they're at the core of all the struggles and emotional upheavals we go through. That's what we call neurosis and what we're working to transform.

The most direct means of relating to these different aspects of neurosis involves working with heightened experiences of the emotions. The more vivid the emotion, the greater the opportunity we have to connect with the experience of wakefulness. There is a classic Buddhist saying: "However strong the emotions are, to that degree the fire of wisdom will blaze." When we connect fully in this way, we're connecting with the basic vibration or energetic aspect of our neurosis, which is beyond conceptual reach. The trust we need to have in order to work with our emotions on this level is not always quick or easy to come by. At this point, it's important for us to recall and connect with the basic principles of emptiness and compassion. That's how we work with our neurosis.

Energized Emptiness, Passionate Compassion

We're no longer talking about emptiness simply in terms of the experience of openness and spaciousness or totality. The direct experience of emptiness at this level has an energized, blissful quality that's part of the experience of fullness. There's a tremendous sense of brilliance and joy. As you've heard several times by now, emptiness is not just empty space like a vacuum; it's not just an experience of nothingness. It's not a magic wand that makes things disappear. On the contrary, it's an experience of brilliant presence that occurs naturally in the absence of fixation, of not holding on to anything. Imagine that something is there, but there's no sense of holding on to it. At the same time, there's a sense of rawness or nakedness, which can be uncomfortable at first. We can use many words to describe the experience of open awareness that goes beyond fixation of any kind, but basically, it's sharp, clear, vibrant, and full of sparks.

When we understand emptiness in this way and can bring that experience together with our ordinary experience of neurosis, it transforms our perception of ourselves and our outlook on the world. Why? In the absence of fixation, our mind becomes free of confusion. We're looking through a clear lens at last. Our blurry picture comes into focus, and we begin to see who we truly are. Instead of regarding ourselves as bewildered and powerless beings in a world of endless confusion, we begin to develop confidence in our own awakened nature and in the awakened nature of everyone with whom we share this world. We have confidence in this, because this is what we now see. We no longer see our neurosis and their neuroses as just workable; we see them as a source of inspiration and enlightenment.

Once we're able to connect with that experience, our practice is to cultivate it, to make that connection again and again. As our confidence grows, we reach the level of affirming that reality, and we see how the experience of fearlessness begins to take place. Not only do we see the possibility of fearlessness, but we also begin to take that fearlessness as the basis for our attitude toward any expression of neurosis. When we can hold that attitude, it's like rebel buddha taking its seat as master of confusion. We can no longer be overwhelmed by powerful emotions; in fact, they only make our world more colorful, more dynamic and awake. We begin to manifest a kind of enlightened pride, a sense of dignity and self-respect that is free of ego.

From this perspective, we can see that emptiness doesn't mean getting away from our hang-ups or making our problems or physical reality disappear. It means seeing beyond our ordinary hang-ups, transcending our fixations. Consequently, there's a total and immediate sense of freedom in emptiness. And when we're free in this way, then what's left is just the experience of brilliance, of spark, which has a tremendous quality of richness.

This sense of enlightened pride, or unshakable confidence in our awakened nature, is a big step toward achieving the full awakening that is total liberation. Now we need to fully join that fearless, open mind with the heart of compassion. When these two are in union, they become the most potent force for overcoming all levels of confusion. But as used here, compassion, too, is somewhat different from our ordinary understanding. It encompasses all the qualities we expect—lovingkindness, sympathetic understanding, and so on—but it goes further. It becomes rawer. It's no longer regarded as just pure kindness in the conventional sense or even kindness in a spiritual sense. The intensity and depth of its feeling has the quality of passion. We are, in a sense, connecting to a primal state of energy and awareness. We're going to the core of our genuine, noble heart, to the most fundamental level of mind: our true, basic being. That journey to the center further strips away our concepts, even what we cling to as virtuous and good. Yet it's full of warmth and gentleness that we can express toward our fellow beings and, most importantly, toward ourselves and our own neurosis. It's a heart inspired by enlightened pride, by the luminosity of this supreme emptiness.

The Union of Emptiness and Compassion

From a Buddhist perspective, compassion is the natural radiance or light of emptiness. These two, emptiness and compassion, are always in union, yet the primordial and powerful nature of this union can be difficult to see. This isn't just an idea, but a reality that seems to be embedded in us and in the very nature of our universe. For example, if you close your eyes, you'll start seeing flashes of light in the darkness. From the Buddhist perspective, that light is not merely an optical phenomenon; the ultimate source of this radiance is the blissful, empty nature of your own mind. In the same way, the light of compassion creates brilliant sparks wherever it manifests, yet the nature of those sparks is always empty. You can see those same sparks in the energy of your emotions, especially in your relationships. Whether you say, "This is love," or "This is hate," there are sparks going on and off all the time that sometimes pull you and someone else together and sometimes push you apart. When you think you want to give the whole thing up and just cash in your chips, you usually just end up with someone else and the whole thing starts over again.

A research physicist I met while traveling told me a story about another kind of relationship that reminded me of this union of emptiness and compassion: the relationship between pairs of quarks. The elementary particles, called "quarks," come in several varieties, such as up and down quarks, which always appear in opposite pairs. If by some means the pair is separated, then out of nowhere, a down quark will spontaneously pop into existence to join the up quark, and an up quark will pop into existence to join the down quark, creating two pairs. Thus, neither the up nor the down quark seems willing or able to exist all by itself, which sounds pretty familiar. How can this be? Empty space is not truly empty; it's actually quite vibrant and full. There is a constant process of transformation taking place: particles transforming into pure energy and pure energy converting back into particle form. In the same way, the relationship of emptiness and compassion is seamless and constant. You'll never find just emptiness or just compassion alone. On this elemental level, they are never divorced. It's a somewhat romantic image—this universe of space and energy as passionate, loving, and selfless all at once.

Compassion's Romantic Heart

As a side effect of working at this primal level of experience, some element of romanticism, of indulgence in the world of the emotions and the senses, comes into play. Why should this be? At its core, compassion is based on passion and desire, an aspect of our nature that we shouldn't fear. Without passion, there would be no love in the world, no commitment to the common cause, no devotion toward enlightened ideals or the thought of awakening. Desire gives rise to longing and aspiration; it moves us to overcome obstacles and achieve great heights. Yet passion and desire in the service of self-interest or bound by fixation and obsession are usually destructive forces in our life. It's safer to stick with ordinary conduct—the performance of good deeds—than to risk working with the romantic aspect of compassion, but that's a bit more superficial.

We began working with our mind by cultivating an attitude of renunciation. Our freedom depended on moving away from all the attachments that kept us bound in states of suffering. Then, through the process of training our mind, we found we could instead use those very attachments and the emotions provoked by them to transform negative mind states into positive ones. Now, having grown up, so to speak, and possessing greater resources of wisdom and compassion, we can meet our mind head-on at its deepest level. Instead of simply abstaining from strong feelings or pleasures, we can look at those states clearly, without confusion.

Usually, when we want something, instead of looking at the desire itself—the pure energy of longing or craving—and connecting to that experience of mind, we fall into ordinary patterns of thought. We miss the original moment, the openness, energy, and brilliance that precedes the start-up of our habitual patterns. That happens over and over, whether our desire is on a grand scale or we simply long for an ice-cold Coke. Thanks to all our thoughts of good and bad, before we even reach for the Coke, we have denied ourselves the pleasure of drinking it. It has too much sugar and too many calories; caffeine is bad; this soda wasn't bottled locally, and so on. Our head says, "Don't drink it," but our taste buds are going, "Mmm." The point is to see our neurosis in all its fullness, in its rawest and most fundamental state, just as it's arising—when we're looking at that can of cold Coke and our whole being is drawn to it. Our passion for that Coke lights up our mind, and there's a moment of wakefulness, pure pleasure, and satisfaction before the onslaught of thought begins. We can fall back asleep in that moment to get away from the intensity and brilliance, or we can back away and pick up some organic carrot juice. Or we can join that moment with enlightened pride, the wisdom of emptiness. Whether we drink the Coke or not is somewhat beside the point; it's a question of how we work with our mind when the desire strikes.

In a sense, we need great passion as a gateway to transcendence. When we join the gentleness and warmth of the naked state of passion with the brilliant spark of emptiness, there's a natural sense of union. The meeting of the two produces the experience of what's called "great bliss wisdom," or great joy. Because all emotions, at their heart, are never separate from compassion, the union of any emotion with emptiness can produce the experience of great joy. With the discovery of this supreme emptiness, the self-existing union of emptiness and compassion, we realize that joy is beginningless and endless. Therefore, we don't need to hold on to it. Like the energy of space, it comes out of nowhere and takes shape for a moment, dissolves, and arises again. There are times when we see it and times when we don't, yet its essence is the same at all times. Space is never less full of energy at one moment than it is at another. At this point, our sense of enlightened pride becomes unwavering. We're not imagining our wakefulness and trying to make ourselves over in that image. We see that we are within a field of wakefulness that includes us. We're a part of something limitless. Our sense of aloneness or individuality is no longer a barrier between us and others. Instead, it's the inspiration for our desire to reach out to others and bring them as much joy and happiness as we can.

We have now come full circle on our journey. Looking back, we can see that first we used the idea of selflessness as a weapon to destroy our confusion. Now we use the experience of selflessness as a source of inspiration and courage to work with our neurosis and the neurosis of the world. When everyone else is trying to climb up out of the depths of suffering, there are a few people going back in. To be such a person requires a lot of bravery and passion for the world. It helps to be a little crazy too.

However, whatever your own path is, wherever it takes you, there is one instruction you should protect and always carry with you: never give up on anyone. Even if you can't help someone now, don't abandon him or her mentally or close the door to your heart. That is the direct word of the Buddha, our ancient revolutionary friend, and if you forget it, you'll hear it again from the mouth of the rebel buddha you're living with right now.

a lineage of awakening

How DO WE preserve a wisdom lineage? Its wisdom must be passed from generation to generation. But there's a difference in preserving a tradition and institutionalizing it. We can fill museums with Buddhist artifacts; we can translate and reproduce texts of past masters and fill the libraries of the world with them; we can document the rituals and codes of its culture. Then no one will be in danger of forgetting Buddhism. It will live on as a fascinating relic, like so many other lost civilizations. On the other hand, we can preserve the wisdom that imbues this tradition by studying and practicing it to the point where we wake up.

This applies to the new generation of practitioners just starting to attend teachings and retreats, as well as to those of you who have been doing that for years and years. I sometimes wonder why some of you are still at it, because I see so little confidence in the possibility of waking up now. Maybe you think you can wake up 50 percent, just enough to get beyond the "crazy" stage but not all the way to "wisdom." However, it's not the message of the Buddha or the intention of Buddhism to provide a partial recovery from confusion. The message of the Buddha is that you're awake now and that you can, if you apply yourself, realize it.

If you live in the West, you might doubt that this message truly applies to you. You might think, "How could I become a realized being? Impossible! How could any Westerner wake up like the Buddha and become a lineage holder? You have to be born into it, like the Asians; it's in their blood." Perhaps you've never thought about it, but even Asians have the same kinds of self-doubt. Once, the enlightened Tibetan yogi Milarepa was approached by a layperson who said, "It's remarkable how you have achieved such realization in just this one lifetime! Such an accomplishment can only be possible because you are a reincarnation of some great being—which buddha or bodhisattva are you an emanation of?" From this perspective, even being Tibetan is not enough. You have to be a superhuman.

In response, Milarepa became extremely upset and said, "By saying that, you are disparaging the Dharma and implying that the path has no power. You are saying that the only reason I can manifest my enlightened nature is because I was born with a head start. You could hardly have a more mistaken view!" In fact, Milarepa started out with a pretty bad record. He had a long list of misdeeds, so he had many obstacles to overcome and had to work very hard. He said, "I practiced Dharma with relentless zeal. Thanks to the profound methods of the path, I developed exceptional qualities. Now, anyone with a bit of determination could develop courage like mine if they had real confidence in the effects of their actions. They would develop the same accomplishments—and then people would think that they were manifestations of a Buddha or great being too."[1]

It's the same for any of us today when we say we can't do it: we're expressing a lack of confidence in the power of the Buddhist path. We doubt that it can produce its advertised result. Yet according to the teachings of great yogis and scholars of the past, it's possible to manifest realization. It's a realistic idea. I'm not talking about a few isolated instances of enlightenment, the liberation of one or two "great" beings sometime in the future. That's not good enough. I'm talking about establishing modern-day lineages of awakening; genuine lineages of American and Western Buddhism can start today. We can see the results in this century.

Every person has the potential to achieve enlightenment. You already have a certain level of intelligence, insight, and compassion that you can develop further, all the way to realization. Trusting that is extremely important. If you lack confidence in yourself, then the experience won't come. If you sit down with the attitude of "Well, I'm sitting, but I know I'm not going to get anywhere today," then you'll probably be right. The best approach is to sit without any expectations, without any hope or fear about the result. Sit with an attitude of openness that admits the possibility instead of shutting the door.

When you compare your cultural upbringing to that of Asian teachers or historical figures of the past, you usually don't see any chance of achieving a realization like theirs. You probably think of yourself as an ordinary, confused person who's a product of a materialistic, dualistic culture, while they have the advantage of being raised from birth under special, even mystical circumstances. Such ideas don't help you; they actually undermine your path.

Think of it in this way: if you were born Jewish or Christian, it means you probably were brought up in a Judeo-Christian environment. Does that give you a special power to realize the nature of God? I think not. It's the same for someone born Hindu, Muslim, or Buddhist. Just being born and raised in a certain culture doesn't guarantee you'll have a profound understanding of that culture's heritage of spiritual teachings. Someone from outside your culture may even have a better, fresher understanding of it.

In fact, if you're born and raised in an Asian Buddhist culture today, you may be more interested to learn Western philosophy, psychology, and technology and look to it for new insights and opportunities. The Buddha is an old, familiar face to you—perhaps too familiar. Even where contemporary Asian Buddhist communities are functioning as practice centers, they face cultural challenges similar to those faced in the West—seeing beyond long-established cultural forms to the heart of the Buddha's teachings. So while we can't speak of establishing Buddhism in Eastern cultures, we can ask, "To what degree are people practicing cultural rituals, and to what degree are they truly waking up?"

That seems to be our common dilemma, East or West. In that sense, we can all go back to look at the example of Prince Siddhartha, whose journey to awakening began when he went outside the boundaries of his own culture. The young Buddha was the quintessential outsider.

The Teacher as Example

The stories we hear about the life of the Buddha and other important figures provide us with inspirational examples. The problem is that we can become confused by the idea of "an example" and exaggerate what the example represents. We also tend to idealize the past. For example, the ruggedness of life in ancient India looks romantic from a distance. Or when we think of the Buddha, we imagine a saintly figure giving out profound teachings. We don't see an Indian man walking dusty paths from village to village; getting hungry, tired, and sore; sometimes smiling and sometimes scowling. Do we think he was meditating all the time? Do we think he never shouted at anyone? He was a human being, just like us, and he can be a wonderful model for us precisely because of that.

The same thing occurs when we look at great yogis from the past. For example, the forefathers of the Tibetan Buddhist lineage are always portrayed as physically perfect, wearing beautiful ornaments, and sitting majestically. They naturally inspire us. However, if we had seen them in person, we would probably have had no idea that they were anyone special or even that they were Buddhist. What were they really like? The father of the Kagyu school, Tilopa, lived for a time as a wandering beggar and fisherman of sorts, who ate the fish guts other fishermen had thrown out. It is said that when his dharma heir, Naropa, first met him, he was eating live fish. Honestly speaking, if Tilopa were sitting in front of us now, it would be very hard for us to relate to him, because we're looking for someone who matches our romantic image of a spiritual master. When we do this, we're not making a heartfelt connection with the path and the teachings of the Buddha.

Another example is Padmasambhava, the Indian man renowned as a "second Buddha," who remains one of the most important and beloved figures in the history of Tibet. Padmasambhava is credited with bringing the dharma to Tibet, and many thousands of Tibetans cherish him and follow his example. But if you read his biography, you will see there were also many in Tibet who hated him and tried to destroy him. They couldn't defeat him because of his spiritual accomplishments, but he inspired enmity as well as devotion.

What these histories demonstrate to us is the human side of these enlightened figures. When we don't see their humanity realistically, we also fail to see their genuine accomplishments. Therefore, we don't benefit from their example. This reminds me of a news report I saw on TV that described how Americans tend to exaggerate the accomplishments and excuse the faults of past presidents but tend to be very critical of the present one. John Lennon said something similar—that you're more loved when you're dead and buried than you are when you're above ground.

Therefore, in relation to the teachers we look to as our examples, it's important for us not to mistake a cultural presentation for a living person. When we look for examples on the path, the examples we find are human ones. Moreover, as my own teacher pointed out to me, it's most important to appreciate the opportunities we have in the present. No matter how kind, intelligent, or wonderful those realized beings of the past may have been, the most kind, generous, and important teachers are our present ones, because they are the only ones we can relate to in person. They're the only ones who can actually know us, give us instructions, and lead us on the path. Buddha Shakyamuni was a wonderful teacher, but you and I can't sit down with him and ask questions about what we should do or how to work with our problems, whereas we can sit down in a coffee shop with our living, flesh-and-blood teacher and talk about our path.

CONTEMPORARY TEACHERS

Who are our present teachers? At this point in time, there is a growing number of contemporary Westerners and Asians who are going through a thorough and rigorous training similar to that which our elder Asian teachers went through. And they're getting similar results. This means that some are becoming wise, skillful, and compassionate teachers in their own right. They're beginning to carry the lineage in an authentic manner, and such teachers should be treated with the same respect as the accomplished teachers who preceded them. They should be trusted equally. Others will go through the training and yet be mediocre or poor teachers, just as there are PhD's who land jobs and get by on their credentials but never produce a single brilliant student because they can't teach what they know. It's the same on the spiritual journey. However, if the Buddha was right, if the mind is awakened and beyond culture, then there are definitely contemporary teachers who will take their seats and guide Buddhism forward in our modern world. This is essential, because the elder generation of Asian teachers we have now won't always be with us. Just as our parents don't live forever, our teachers pass away. Hopefully, we'll have learned from them what we need to know in order to live a compassionate and meaningful life and to carry forward the lineage of awakening.

My advice in this regard is to examine all your teachers and accept whoever possesses the qualities of wisdom, compassion, and skill, regardless of where they come from. However, just as in any culture or tradition—even old Tibet was no exception—today's Buddhism will see some self-proclaimed "masters" who are charlatans. There seems to be no shortage of charlatans in any spiritual scene. It's important for students to distinguish between such pretenders and genuine teachers and to always follow a genuine holder of the Buddha's lineage.

You, the students of today living in Vancouver and New York, London and Hamburg, Barcelona and Hong Kong, are the teachers of tomorrow. Even if that's not in your game plan at the moment, it may happen. That's how it works. So as a potential teacher yourself, you must trust your capacity to learn and embody genuine wisdom. Students today have many advantages. You start your practice with a good education and an impressive range and depth of knowledge. Therefore, in many ways, you're intellectually prepared for a journey whose goal is transcendent knowledge. Capacity or potential is not the problem. The challenge is to discriminate what is culture and what is wisdom—which is an old problem, it turns out.

CULTURAL PRESSURES: A HANDFUL OF DUST

There's a famous story in *The Words of My Perfect Teacher* by Patrul Rinpoche—one of the most illustrious teachers of the nineteenth century—about a well-known twelfth-century Kadampa teacher called Geshe Ben. The story goes that Geshe Ben was expecting a visit from a large number of his benefactors and some students. On the morning of their expected arrival, he set about arranging the offerings on his shrine.

He was absorbed in making his shrine very impressive, when suddenly he had a realization. In the next moment, he picked up a handful of dust and threw it all over the offerings. When this incident was told to the great Indian master, Padampa Sangye, he said, "That handful of dust that Geshe Ben threw was the best offering in all Tibet."[2] This is a shocking story for us. Can you imagine throwing dust on a shrine?

Why did Geshe Ben first beautify his shrine and then throw dust all over it? He was a great practitioner, so it was more than just an ego-centered desire to impress his benefactors. There was a cultural tradition that put tremendous pressure on him. It would have been regarded as disrespectful not to clean and arrange his shrine and set out extra special offerings. However, in the middle of his preparations, he realized that he had no heart connection to his actions, no sense of inspiration, and worst of all, no sense of mindfulness or awareness. Therefore, he picked up a handful of dust and threw it on the shrine, saying, "Monk, just stay where you are, and don't put on airs."

More recently, we have the story of Gendun Choephel, a great but famously unconventional teacher, scholar, and translator, who lived in the first half of the twentieth century. One day, two very learned scholars from the universities of two famous monasteries came to talk to Gendun Choephel, but their visit was more than a social call. They had been hearing stories about his crazy behavior, so they came to check up on him—to "help" him, so to speak. When he heard that they were coming to see him, Gendun Choephel took out his most precious Buddha statue and set it on the table. Then he rolled up a Tibetan hundred-dollar bill and made it into a cigarette. When the scholars arrived, he lit the cigarette and started smoking it. They looked at his cigarette and saw that it was a real hundred-dollar bill. Then, as he was smoking, Gendun Choephel tapped the ashes on the Buddha statue, and the scholars couldn't stand this. It was okay that he wasted his hundred dollars, but they couldn't stand the idea of him tapping the cigarette ashes on the statue of the Buddha. They then launched into a great debate and argument with Gendun Choephel, but in the end, they could not defeat his view that one's sense of respect for the Buddha and heart connection to his teachings are all very much within. "Buddha" is nothing outside. Furthermore, if Buddha is completely enlightened, beyond duality and concept, would he be bothered by a few cigarette ashes? He would not.

These stories remind us that we can get so caught up in the cultural forms of dharma that we begin to go against the heart of our spiritual path. Both stories show great teachers "throwing dust" on objects we generally regard as sacred. But instead of desecrating these objects, there's a sense of being liberated from our concepts of good and bad, pure and impure, beautiful and ugly. These concepts are the source of the tremendous cultural pressures to abide by certain rules, whether explicit or unspoken. If we don't follow the rules, then we feel extremely uncomfortable and may be ostracized. But when we do follow the rules, even mindlessly, without any genuine understanding of our actions, then we look very good from the outside. We may even fool ourselves for a while.

When we're just going through the motions, our actions don't have much meaning. We're like workers on an assembly line at a big auto factory, where people are lined up doing just one thing over and over. They don't have to think about it. They might even forget about what they're making. If their job is to install a single screw, they just do it. When a certain part comes near, they install the screw. In a similar way, we can lose track of the purpose of our actions and become assembly-line workers of liberation. We go through all the prescribed motions, but nothing gets through to us. We don't really see our shrine or even remember what's on it, let alone what it represents. We don't appreciate the spaciousness and energy of our sitting. We're not changed by the words we read. We may have accumulated many Buddhist statues, books, and all the trappings of a meditator's life to the degree that our home looks like a giant spiritual mall. But after collecting all these things, we forget that we have them. We might even buy the same book two or three times, not realizing that we already have a copy.

There may be some things worth collecting, like baseball cards or antiques, because one day we might see a return on our investment. However, from the spiritual point of view, there's no point to our actions if we're doing something mindlessly. There is no liberation if we're not aware. There is no joy if we're not connecting with our heart. So when mindfulness and awareness are missing in any action, what good is it from the point of view of buddhadharma? Losing this heart connection is not just a liability for us individually; it can affect a practice community or an entire tradition.

SCARECROW DHARMA

The revolution of mind instigated by the Buddha didn't happen just once. The buddhadharma has gone through many periods of revolution and change. This is necessary, because it's natural for some level of degeneration, misinformation, or confusion to creep into any system over time. Just as we need to regularly run programs that scan our computers for viruses and malware, we need to continually review, refine, and refresh our spiritual systems. In Buddhism, we have a history of doing that.[3]

Therefore, what we're talking about here—revolutionizing the dharma—isn't something new at all. This has been going on in Buddhist culture for twenty-six hundred years. When a living tradition becomes static, without any sense of freshness, and we lose our basic heart connection with the spiritual journey, it's actually very sad. The dharma is no longer the real, genuine dharma at all. Buddha called this condition a "symbol of dharma." It's only a form, like a scarecrow. A scarecrow looks like a human. It has everything—head, arms, hands, legs, and feet. It wears a hat, a coat, trousers, boots, and sometimes sunglasses. It seems like everything's there. It looks like a real person, but it's just a scarecrow, just a symbol.

We need to watch out for scarecrow dharma. We could be in a grand meditation hall, where there's a beautiful shrine, a teacher, a teaching, an assembly of students, and a cultural practice. Everything looks perfect and complete. We may feel that we're in an ideal dharmic situation, but it can still be scarecrow dharma. That's the dangerous part. Buddha himself says in his teachings that the dharma will never be destroyed by outer conditions. The only thing that can destroy the dharma comes from within. Therefore, not looking at what's going on inside can be much more destructive than worrying about unfavorable external conditions.

No matter what kind of forms we're considering, there should be a heart connection, a genuine understanding of these elements of our path. There should be a sincere sense of dedication that comes from our confidence in our understanding. Without that, our experience of the path becomes scarecrow dharma; it's not the real thing.

What Buddha Taught

After his enlightenment, Buddha Shakyamuni taught for forty-five years. All in all, there's a vast literature that is in the process of being translated from source languages into English and other Western languages. Sometimes it is said that there are eighty-four thousand dharmas or teachings of the Buddha. But in fact, it's equally true to say that the Buddha taught only one thing, one single, profound instruction: how to work with your mind.

To work with your mind means to work with your thoughts, emotions, and basic sense of self-clinging, all of which exist formlessly. They don't speak any particular language or wear the national dress of a particular country. So these are universal experiences of mind. Therefore, there's no cultural diversity in our emotions. Anger is anger. There isn't a Tibetan form of anger and an American form of anger. There may be different cultural styles of expressing or repressing anger, but the internal experience is the same. When you get angry, no words can describe it; it doesn't matter which language you speak. Anger just vibrates in your body, and your mind goes blank. In the same way, there's no cultural form of ego. No matter where you come from, there's a fundamental sense of "I" that is the same for everyone. There isn't one sense of "I" for people in New Delhi and another form for people in Los Angeles. Furthermore, the basic state of suffering seems to manifest everywhere, without allegiance to any country or culture. Fortunately or unfortunately, the human race shares at least these experiences, in which there are no barriers or differences between us.

In the same way, the experience of being awake is alike for everyone.

It's an experience of mind that transcends culture. Wisdom that brings the experience of awakening must also be universal, or every country would need its own "buddha" for its citizens. If there is an Asian nature of mind that's different from an American or European or African nature of mind, then we would have to conclude that there's no point in teaching the wisdom of the Buddha anywhere but in Asia. We could all save ourselves a lot of time, money, and headaches by admitting it. Yet when we look around us, we see that wisdom, too, manifests everywhere. It seems to have no favorites. East or West—same sleep, same suffering; same waking, same happiness.

Going Forward: What to Rely On

With all the different teachers and teachings we are exposed to these days, how do we know who to listen to and which teachings we can have confidence in? The Buddha addressed the question of spiritual authority in a teaching that came to be called the Four Reliances. These Four Reliances can help us develop a better understanding of our way forward in this culture and at this time. He said,

> Rely on the teaching, not the person.
> Rely on the meaning, not the words.
> Rely on the definitive meaning, not the provisional meaning.
> Rely on wisdom, not on consciousness.[4]

We should make a poster of these instructions and hang it everywhere: in our living room, kitchen, bedroom, bathroom, on the floors and ceilings. They are that important. When we practice these Four Reliances, we can have confidence that we're on the right path and that we'll receive the full benefit of it.

First Reliance: Rely on the Teaching

When the Buddha says, "Rely on the teaching, not the person," this means that we shouldn't be fooled by appearances. The teacher may be very attractive, come from an illustrious family, and ride in a limousine with many attendants. Conversely, he or she may look quite ordinary and live in humble circumstances. Whether the teacher is Asian or Western, male or female, young or old, conventional or unconventional, famous or unknown, you can judge how qualified and reliable a teacher is by looking at the quality and effectiveness of his or her instructions, degree of insight and realization, and lineage connections. This is important, because there have been many worthy teachers whose appearance and lifestyles didn't match their students' expectations. Therefore, you should rely more on the teaching than on what you think or feel about the person who gives it.

Second Reliance: Rely on the Meaning

Here the Buddha's message, "Rely on the meaning, not the words," is that we should rely for guidance on the meaning that's being pointed out and not just on our conceptual understanding of the words. Meaning is carried by words but is not the words themselves. If we get caught at the level of words, we may think that our conceptual understanding is ultimate, a true experience of realization. But we should understand that words are like the finger that points at the moon. If we look only at the finger, we remain at the level of concept. We will only fully understand the meaning of the words when we stop looking at the finger and turn toward the moon. We do this by reflecting deeply on what we've heard, until our reflections carry us beyond the words to a more direct and personal experience of their meaning. You'll only know what Earl Grey tea is by drinking the tea in your cup. You'll only know what emptiness is by discovering the experience within yourself.

Third Reliance: Rely on the Definitive Meaning

With "rely on the definitive meaning, not the provisional meaning," the Buddha is pointing out that we need to know not only the meaning of words but also when a meaning is "definitive" and when it is "provisional." That's another way of saying that some meanings are ultimate and some are relative. An ultimate meaning is final and complete— that's the way it truly is, and there's nothing more to be said about that topic. A relative meaning may be an important and powerful understanding, but it's not final or complete; it's something that's intended to lead us further. We learn many relative truths on our way to understanding the ultimate truth. For example, when Buddha taught the truth of suffering, it helped lead people to the path that freed them from suffering. However, suffering is relative in nature; it doesn't exist in the ultimate nature of mind. What does exist is selflessness, compassion, joy, wakefulness, and so forth. That is mind's ultimate nature. In the third reliance, the Buddha is saying to rely on meanings that are definitive or ultimate. If we tried to hold on to our belief in suffering as an ultimate truth, then we could never experience the joy of being free from suffering.

Fourth Reliance: Rely on Wisdom

Here the Buddha is saying that in order to directly experience and comprehend the definitive, or ultimate, meaning we're talking about, we need to rely on wisdom—mind's capacity to know in a nonconceptual way—and not on our dualistic consciousness. When we say, "consciousness," we're talking about relative mind: the appearances of the five sense perceptions and the conceptual, thinking mind. What is their relationship to wisdom? They're the manifestation and play of wisdom itself. As vivid as they are, these appearances have no solid existence. However, until we recognize that, it can be difficult to see the wisdom inherent in all our experiences, especially our thoughts and emotions. So how do we practice this reliance? Once we understand this intellectually, we need to develop more confidence in it and make it part of our ordinary experience. For example, when a thought arises, we remind ourselves that it's just a thought. If it's an angry thought, a wish to harm someone, we can use that very thought to make a connection to wisdom, first on a relative level. If we mix our anger with the thought of compassion, then that changes the signal we're sending in a fundamental way. It brings a sense of openness and heart connection that may allow for a better relationship in the future. So until we're able to connect with ultimate wisdom, it's important to remember to connect with the qualities of relative wisdom—a simple sense of openness and compassion for ourselves and others. When we can do that, we're relying on wisdom and not on consciousness.

building community

HEART ADVICE OF THE BUDDHA

BEFORE THE BUDDHA passed away, his students asked how they should continue their community, which relied on many rules of conduct as well as teachings for working with mind. The Buddha said that after he was gone, the Buddhist community should continue "in accordance with the times and the society." He was saying that the Buddhist community should change as needed in order to remain contemporary and relate harmoniously with society. This is the heart advice of the Buddha.

In order to see the way forward, we have to see where we are now, which means we have to see our own culture. It's not just some other people who have cultural habits and attachments, customs and points of view. We have to see that culture exists on both sides. Whether we come from the American or Asian side, we can be like fish swimming in the ocean. Fish see everything that's in the ocean, but they don't see themselves or the water they're swimming in. In the same way, we can easily see the habits and customs of others, but we can remain blind to our own. As we become more conscious of our cultural environment, we begin to see how we put our world together. We start to recognize how we construct culture and identity with mind, and how mind labels everything and stamps it with values. Once we see this connection, we're seeing the water itself, the unbiased wakefulness that pervades our experience. We need this kind of clarity in order to avoid becoming simply importers and exporters of culture. There may be a market for it, but that's not what we're here for. It could be our livelihood, but it's not our spiritual path.

So how will contemporary Buddhism evolve, and what will it look like? If we take Buddha at his word, then we can relax and allow time for Buddhism and our various cultures to mix. Nevertheless, the "look" of Buddhism, the forms that organically arise as we bring our understanding into our human activity, will be different in Poland than in Peru, for example, where youthful but strong Buddhist communities are now developing. We often want to know, "Are we getting it right?" As long as the essence of Buddhism, its wisdom, is at the heart of any cultural form of Buddhism, it can be correct for that time and place.

Buddhism in America

We could say that Buddhism develops its mature cultural identity in a way that's similar to the spiritual path of an individual. American Buddhism is going through that process now. First there was a period of basic training, when everyone was just learning what Buddhism was and how to be a Buddhist of any kind at all. During this period, everyone tended to follow closely the forms and practices of their particular school. Being an "American Buddhist" was not anyone's worry yet. Buddhist groups were somewhat isolated from the general community in the beginning. Then, after a few decades, Buddhism and Buddhists began to become more integrated with their communities and to look and feel more like them. These days, it's not as easy to spot Buddhists on the street by what they're wearing. Now we're in the period of simply being who we are and appreciating our American way of being neurotic as well as awake.

We seem to be at the point where our Buddhism and our Americanism can come together. Hopefully, as we take this step, we can go beyond cultural and spiritual sectarianism and become a voice of reason and compassion in our society. Traditional Buddhism and our youthful American Buddhism may not always look like they're on the same page. This may be the cause of occasional distress, but then parents always worry about their kids, and kids always think they know more and are cooler than their parents. But every generation is new and has to make its own discoveries about this journey. The further they go on their own path, the more proud and respectful they'll be of the family history. That's life in any family, isn't it?

So here we are, changing and being changed. Buddhist organizations today have already been transformed by their encounter with American culture. Students may come to dharma centers to learn Eastern philosophy and the practice of meditation, but the minute they walk through the door, they bring America with them. With their understanding of business management, organizational development, law, and finance, these students are helping to create healthy, democratic, and sustainable dharma centers. Other students are plugging their centers into the Internet, creating beautiful design work, translating, publishing, leading classes, and arranging social events. A dharma center is not necessarily a place just for contemplative activities any longer. It can be a full-fledged community for learning of all kinds, with social activities for young and old and families with children. This is a departure from traditional dharma organizations, but this transition is critically important for Buddhism to be viable in America.

We need to see the American face of Buddha's teachings in contemporary society. This also means that we need to see what Buddhist wisdom shares with other wisdom traditions and with the innate wisdom that is everybody's birthright. We all need to step out of a mind-set that sees one kind of wisdom here and another kind there. My students will tell me that they've read something or seen a movie that they're excited about because "it's very Buddhist" without being Buddhist. They're constantly educating me on American culture. They send me books, CDs, and links to websites. It doesn't matter if something comes from the East or West, if it's ancient wisdom or cutting-edge technology. They want to know more about it if it says something relevant to their lives. It may be about how the mind works or how to go "green" or how to start a business. They're showing me every day how worldly life and the spiritual path start to become one. We've been talking about this all along, but it's another matter to do it. If we can get over our idea that wisdom is exclusive to certain people or groups, then our world expands dramatically.

Buddha Then and Now

What would the Buddha be thinking and doing if he were alive today? He would probably be talking with neuroscientists and physicists and the theorists of consciousness studies. These scientists are the ones asking questions like those the Buddha asked long ago, only they're using the language of biology, math, and philosophy. If such a meeting were to take place, we might hear some interesting new teachings from the Buddha. On the other hand, we might benefit from the development of new scientific theories. For ourselves, at this time, we should ask how the research data coming out of these fields might impact our Buddhist worldview and what we do on the cushion. This knowledge didn't exist in these forms during the time of the Buddha. On the other hand, what role does science play at the point where concept stops and laboratory-style observation and measurement become impossible? In any case, the meeting of science and Buddhism that is going on today is producing an East-West dialogue that's tremendously rich and provocative. It's a dialogue that continues to push at the boundary between the known and unknown, or relative and absolute truth. It's not that anyone expects reality to change as a result, but certainly our knowledge about it is increasing in dramatic and instructive ways.

However, knowledge that's not put to use in the service of compassion benefits only the knowledge holders, which is a waste of wisdom. One of the greatest contributions we can make to our world is to learn how to live in harmony with each other. In his lifetime, the Buddha was very concerned with the creation of a harmonious community, and the hundreds of monastic rules he established were created, not only to help individual monks and nuns achieve their own liberation, but also to promote nonviolent and harmonious living conditions. Our modern Buddhist communities aren't retreat centers or monasteries, but we can still have the same goal, if not the same rules.

So "in accordance with the times and the society," if the Buddha were with us today, he might send us all to get training in group dynamics, team building, and conflict resolution. He might also send us to psychologists to help us deal with our personal issues—so he didn't have to hear about them all the time and to prevent them from spilling over into the lives of our families and communities. Being good meditators doesn't necessarily mean that we have the good communication or interpersonal skills we need to get along with others. If we lack these skills, then we should think about getting trained in them. We'll never develop stable, harmonious communities if we constantly have to say to each other, "That's not what I meant!" At the same time, we can contribute our understanding of the benefits of meditation and mindfulness-awareness training to these educational systems.

Whatever is helpful to us in working with our minds and emotions can be a part of our path, when we include it with the practice of mindfulness and meditation. It's all part of learning to be awake, aware human beings who can contribute something meaningful to our world. Throughout Buddhist history, the arts have always been considered an important way to work with our emotions and share our human experience at the same time—our happiness and sadness, joys and sorrows. Our mind is naturally creative, although sometimes we block that creativity. When we train ourselves in one of the arts, we're learning to apply a sense of discipline to our emotions; yet at the same time, we're nurturing our creativity and intuitive wisdom. Moreover, art that is performed onstage has a special power to communicate to an audience. When that connection is made, the people in the audience are not separate from the artists. They become artists, too, in a way. A kind of mind-body synchronization takes place between the audience and the artists on stage.

The point is that whatever our occupation or interests may be, we can make our path a way of life and our life a basis for expressing our wisdom and compassion in the world. The Buddha himself was not just interested in ultimate truth and the liberation of individuals from their suffering. He thought deeply about the welfare of society, and his teachings reflect the connection between the development of the individual and social institutions of all kinds. He taught that we must begin our spiritual journey by working with ourselves and developing our own understanding. Then, step-by-step, we reach a level of realization in which we can open our hearts to all living beings. In this way, the progressive development of the individual becomes the basis for the development of social harmony and cohesion.

In lesser-known secular teachings, the Buddha laid out a system of social organization based on democratic principles that's amazing in its detail and scope. He discussed methods for the election of a head of state, the qualifications of various leaders, and their duties to care for their people. He spoke of how to create a stable economy that would protect against unemployment and food shortages and provide sufficient shelter and means of communication to its citizens. He even described the situation in which a government could properly take over or "bail out" distressed entities whose wealth was integral to the economic health of the nation. He declared it the responsibility of the state to educate its citizens and to overcome partisanship and bring people of different religious and philosophical beliefs together in a state of true cooperation. He also discussed the need for a strong and vigilant military to protect the life and property of the state's citizens. And he advocated the establishment of an equitable and purposeful judiciary that would enforce laws, yet in a manner intended to improve the conduct of criminals. In all of these areas, the guiding principles were loving-kindness, compassion, generosity, and selflessness.[1]

According to the Buddha, we are all fundamentally equal, regardless of social standing, wealth, ethnicity, race, gender, or whom we love. The only basis of judgment is our actions. Therefore, in the Buddhist world, there should be no glass ceiling to break through. There should be no immigration quotas or second-class citizens. If the communities we're developing are not truly open and inclusive, they won't be strong, vibrant, or enduring. On the other hand, we're not trying to appeal to this or that demographic, like politicians trying to expand their base. We're not going for the biggest market share of "the spiritually interested" to fill seats at programs and buy our T-shirts. We're not looking for anything artificial at all. We're simply trying to be genuine people who aspire to reach out to our world. If that's not enough, then we have nowhere to go as followers of the Buddha—in America or anywhere else.

Throwing Out Our Cultural Cushions

The pioneers of Western Buddhism had to overcome certain barriers in order to make sense of this "new" tradition and practice it. They were not only meeting a foreign culture, they were also meeting alien concepts like selflessness and emptiness that made little sense to the Western mind. But they said yes to meditation and working with ego. Now, roughly fifty years later, it's time for a change. We're stuck at a certain level of our spiritual development. What at first woke us up now barely stirs us from our thoughts. What supported our inquiry into who we are now blocks our realization of that. Now we have to ask ourselves how to break through again. This time we're challenged to break through our attachment to all that brought us to this point—the spiritual cultures that we so respect and emulate that they've become another trap for us.

You may say, "That's not my problem. Someone else may be doing that, but I'm not that stupid." If that's your view, then I would say, "Look again." We're still collectively dragging old forms and ideas into the present. Without even noticing it, we're walking down the street wearing the clothes and paraphernalia of another time and place—metaphorically, at least. The reason we do this is because we still think spirituality is "over there." We don't think spirituality is right here with us, in our everyday life. That's why we dream of going to Asia or finding someone called a guru.

When the Buddha awakened, he was sitting on a cushion of grass under a tree in a forest. There was nothing particularly sacred around him; he wasn't doing anything but looking at his mind. All that he had was his experience in life and his understanding of how to work with his mind. His only other possessions were his determination and his confidence that he could deal with whatever occurred in his mind and transform it into a path of awakening.

I've often told students to go outside and meditate—sit on a park bench, breathe in the fresh air, look up in the sky! It's so beautiful. Many find this difficult, though, because they think they're not in a "practice atmosphere." They're without their shrine, their Buddha, their cushions, and their meditation bibles. When it comes to practicing at home, it doesn't occur to them that they can sit on the chair passed down from their grandmother or a pillow they bought from IKEA. They think, "I need a Japanese zafu or a Tibetan gomden, the standardized ones with the correct dimensions from an official meditation supplier. Without these, I can't meditate!" In that case, I guess that the time we spend in a grocery store or driving a car or doing anything else is inferior to the time we spend doing our "real" practice in the shrine room. But please explain to me, what is the difference between your driving mind, your shopping mind, and your sitting mind? Do you have different kinds of thoughts and emotions?

When we adopt too many aspects of the culture we're learning from, we can begin to feel pressured by it. We stop relating to situations with any immediacy. Instead, we relate to what's happening in front of us through a filter of rules and regulations. Especially in the shrine room, there's the sense of an unspoken rule. If we don't follow that rule, we feel extremely uncomfortable. The teacher comes in, and we bow. That's a rule. We would be shocked if we were asked to do something different. We would feel like we were doing something wrong. Nevertheless, we don't see the actual person walking in; we don't make contact because we're already thinking, "Oh, he's a great reincarnated being. He was recognized before his birth and trained in such and such a way." That's our conceptual bullshit.

If we look like Buddhists and talk like Buddhists and sit on a cushion like all the other Buddhists, then we think we are automatically followers of the Buddha's teachings. But all of these concepts are cutting us off from the utter simplicity of the Buddha's example and message. We do what we do simply to wake up, simply to be free. Any form we use is only a support for accomplishing that purpose. We could be perfect in the performance of a thousand rituals, and they could all be empty of meaning and benefit if we don't connect with our heart. If we're not developing our awareness in our everyday life, then we're missing the point.

A genuine lineage of American or Western Buddhism within any particular contemporary culture can develop only when we have a direct connection to the teachings—one that's personal and experiential and brings us back to our own life, our own mind. This will only be possible by breaking through this shell of blockages that we've built up layer by layer out of these cultural traditions. We're not talking about simply changing one form for another form. That's not change. That would be more like a corporate takeover, like Visa taking over MasterCard, which would only mean that our bills would arrive with a different logo. We're also not talking about simply ignoring all aspects of Asian spiritual culture and hoping that there will be something left that can become Western Buddhism. It's not just by ignoring another culture's forms that you evolve your own tradition.

What frees us from being stuck? What cuts through our psychological blockages? We need the courage of our rebel buddha heart to leap beyond forms, to go deeper into our practice and find a way to trust ourselves. We must become our own guide. Ultimately, no one else can lead us through the landscape of our own life. When we stand up in this way, we're not isolated from all that's come before us. The past becomes a true support for the first time, instead of a drag. We're buoyed up by its wisdom and energy, yet the open space ahead of us is ours to navigate. It's an adventure. What we do has purpose and meaning: our discoveries bring us a true sense of freedom and eventually become a support for other travelers. This is the way we untie the knots that bind us and evolve a genuinely contemporary and relevant tradition, along with the forms of its expression.

If we can't do that, then maybe we should start fresh. We could throw out all of our cushions and all of our spiritual trappings, including our clinging to our identity as Buddhists, and begin again by simply sitting in an empty room with completely white walls. This may sound extreme, but we're at one extreme already—too much culture! For the time being, it may be best to swing to the opposite end of the spectrum, the extreme of "no culture," and then slowly come back to a middle ground. Sometimes going to an extreme is the only way to trigger a revolution of mind. If we tried to move directly from our extreme attachment to culture to a place where culture and nonattachment can coexist, then we'd always have room to interpret: "Yes, I'm sitting in my shrine room. Yes, I'm bowing as I enter and leave. But I'm not attached to any of it." It's hard to break old habits. We always go back to our comfortable clinging. It's too easy to return to that spot and interpret it as being a culture-free zone. However, if we're thrown to the other extreme, then there's no room for interpretation because there's no form to cling to. We don't have to worry about being stuck there, because our habitual tendencies will start pulling us back in the other direction, like a powerful magnet. We may swing back and forth for a while, but eventually the oscillation between these two poles will slow down and stop in the middle. This approach leads to the discovery of the middle path.

That is exactly what the Buddha did so long ago. His discovery of a middle path beyond all extremes led to his final breakthrough, his liberation from all misunderstanding into the space of complete wakefulness. We can remember his example and try to follow it. That's why we have an image of the Buddha where we practice sitting and looking directly at our mind. The Buddha is not an object of worship but of inspiration. Remembering him is like looking in a mirror. We look in mirrors every day to comb our hair, shave our beard, or put on makeup. But in this case, we're looking to try to see our true self, the face of our enlightenment. Looking in this way sends a message. It's like saying to ourselves, "Yes, you're a buddha too. You have the same enlightened potential. You can wake up any minute, just like Shakyamuni Buddha and many others." Therefore, when we remember the Buddha, what we're doing is trying to see our own awakened nature. We're trying to see how all of these teachings exist in our everyday life: taking piano lessons, driving our kids to school, walking home from a bar, or locking ourselves up in a three-year retreat—they're all the same.

We remember the path that leads to that awakening by recalling the Buddha's teachings, and we remember, too, the lineage of people who have traveled that path—and are traveling it now—all the way to freedom. When we remember them, it gives us courage, because we see that enlightenment is not just a historical event that happened once, thousands of years ago. Enlightenment is living today in the form of great teachers and communities of dedicated practitioners, East and

West. They, too, are mirrors of enlightenment, in which we can see our own face. When we see in this way, we go beyond duality. There is no subject or object in that moment of openness; there is no difference between their minds and our mind, between their enlightenment and our enlightenment. The two become one.

editor's note

REBEL BUDDHA is the result of the coming together of two lecture series on dharma and culture presented almost ten years apart. The first lectures were given by Dzogchen Ponlop Rinpoche, in the fall of 1999, to the Nalandabodhi sangha in Boulder, Colorado. Surprisingly direct and colorful, they challenged the young sangha to "leap beyond" mere cultural forms of spiritual practice to realize the formless wisdom at their core. A decade later, in the summer of 2008, Rinpoche addressed a large gathering of his Nalandabodhi students at Nalanda West, Center for American Buddhism, in Seattle, Washington. Over a period of ten days, he described the Buddhist spiritual journey in terms so ordinary and free of Buddhist vocabulary that it was some days before those present realized what they were hearing: a precise rendering of the spiritual journey that focused on the internal experience of the traveler rather than its philosophic underpinnings. These lectures brought to mind the excitement and immediacy of the "Boulder Talks," and it was only a matter of months before the idea of combining the two in book form was decided and *Rebel Buddha* was born.

Rinpoche was actively involved in the editorial process from beginning to end. He guided the overall organization of the book, starting with the development of the outline. The contents of the two lecture series were supplemented with excerpts from Rinpoche's other teachings, in particular, certain descriptions of the nature of mind and the instructions for meditation, which were given at different times. Because of Rinpoche's travel schedule, I sent each draft to him by e-mail. Periodically, I would read him sections of the book over the telephone—or in person if he was in Seattle. During the live readings, he would give directions for changes, make corrections, and sometimes dictate new text. He did it all very quickly, seemingly without thought. He invariably insisted that the language of the book should be the ordinary speech of everyday life so that anyone interested in a spiritual path could pick it up and get something out of it.

In addition, during the course of working on the manuscript, Rinpoche not only engaged in lively conversation about culture and dharma with myself and others, but he also took delight in pointing out the genuine dharma that is naturally present in our day-to-day lives, as well as the false, "scarecrow dharma" he saw at times when we adopted our "good Buddhist" personas. In response to a student's question, he might answer with a recently scribed poem, a quote from Albert Einstein or Jimi Hendrix, or a rock song from his iPod. All of these types of exchanges—direct, indirect, and enigmatic—helped to inform and shape the contents of this book.

After spending a year or so—which is not much time for creating a book—reading and organizing this cycle of teachings, I'm still impressed by the enormous amount of information contained in so few words: a contemplation on culture, a full description of the Buddhist path, and well-considered advice and encouragement on how to build a Buddhist community and establish a genuine lineage of awakening in the spiritually fertile West. I'm enormously grateful to Rinpoche for these teachings and for the opportunity to have worked with them. I'm inconceivably happy to see them go forth into the world.

Cindy Shelton
Nalanda West, Seattle, Washington

editor's acknowledgments

I AM GRATEFUL to the many individuals who, collectively, have created the auspicious conditions for the appearance of *Rebel Buddha,* Dzogchen Ponlop Rinpoche's unique and inspiring contemplation on the Buddhist spiritual journey and its encounter with the West. First, acknowledgments and thanks are due to the students of Nalandabodhi, Rinpoche's network of meditation and study centers. Rinpoche first presented these teachings at Nalandabodhi Boulder, Colorado, and Seattle, Washington, and Nalandabodhi members recorded, transcribed, and archived all lectures. Pat Lee, Dave Vitello, and Robert Fors recorded the teachings at Nalanda West; Heather Chan and Megan Johnston transcribed them; and Ayesha and Collin Rognlie maintain Rinpoche's archive. Also, Heather Chan and Gerry Wiener kindly made their extensive notes from the Seattle lectures available. I'm especially grateful for the ongoing advice and assistance of Nalandabodhi's excellent teachers and translators; in particular, Tyler Dewar offered insightful editorial suggestions, and Karl Brunnholzl provided "technical support" in the form of scholarly guidance. My appreciation also goes to Michael Miller and Diane Gregorio, the Nalandabodhi chairpersons, for their support and assistance in making Rinpoche's work available to the world.

A special mention is due to Ceci Miller, to whom I am deeply indebted for editorial assistance. Ceci reviewed and commented on each draft of the manuscript with intelligence, sensitivity, and lightning speed. She helped *Rebel Buddha* become the book it was intended to be. I'm also grateful to Dennis Hunter for his detailed reading of the text and astute editorial suggestions. Thank you to Stephanie Johnston, an informed and reliable reader, for helpful notes. For environmental support and wise counsel, thank you to Mary Chung, Carlos Ferreyros, Marty Marvet, Lynne Conrad Marvet, Tim Walton, Midori McColskey, and Mark Power. A special thanks to Robert Fors for his daily kindnesses and support of Rinpoche's activities.

Thank you to William Clark for representing Rinpoche's book with both skill and grace. I'm grateful to Peter Turner and Sara Bercholz of Shambhala Publications for their support of this book and confidence in its vision. It has been my pleasure to work with Rinpoche's editor at Shambhala, Emily Bower. I have much to thank Emily for—her indisputable editorial skills, patience, encouragement, and guidance.

My deepest thanks to Dzogchen Ponlop Rinpoche, who guided the development of this book at every step and continues to teach me the big lessons in life—one of which is the importance of details. In books and in our spiritual lives, overlook nothing! You may be surprised by what it is that wakes you up. Finally, thank you to rebel buddha, who was behind this from the beginning and will be with us until the end.

Cindy Shelton

appendix 1

INSTRUCTIONS FOR MEDITATION PRACTICE

THE PRACTICE of meditation is basically a process of getting to know yourself by becoming familiar with your mind. The Buddhist view of the mind is that it's always awake. Its nature is awareness and compassion. To discover and enjoy the mind's nature fully, the Buddha taught various methods of meditation. Whatever meditation practices we may do, they are all intended to increase our mindfulness and awareness, strengthen our sense of inner peace, and improve our ability to deal with our emotions as well.

Calm abiding meditation, or shamatha, is a practice that helps us to develop a peaceful state of mind, along with the ability to remain in a peaceful state for increasing periods of time. Normally our mind is a whirlwind of thought, so "peace" is the calming down of the mental agitation and stress caused by this whirlwind.

Not only are our minds busy thinking, our thoughts are usually aimed backward or forward, as we relive past events or obsessively imagine and prepare for the future. We usually don't experience the present moment at all. As long as this process continues, our mind never comes to rest. It's difficult to feel any sense of contentment or satisfaction living in a remembered past or in a future that's mostly projection and speculation. If we ever do arrive at a moment we've imagined, we're already preparing for another future—a better, brighter one.

The first form of calm abiding, or sitting meditation, slows or cools down this whirlwind of thought. When sitting meditation is practiced over time, the mind begins to fall naturally into a resting state, which allows us to be fully present in our life. When we're not being pulled into the past or future, we can relax and begin to genuinely experience the present moment.

Meditation helps us to be successful at the two other kinds of training—discipline and higher knowledge—as well. All three depend on our ability to focus on our path, to see clearly what we're doing, and to understand why we're doing it. We practice all three trainings so that we can free ourselves of the habitual patterns and misconceptions that cause us to suffer and keep that suffering going.

Following are instructions for a recommended meditation posture and for three types of sitting meditation—two based on observing the breath, and one based on observing an external object.

SITTING MEDITATION

To begin a session of sitting meditation, you first need a comfortable seat. You can use any cushion firm enough to support an upright posture. You can also sit in a chair. The main point is to have a relaxed but erect posture, so that your spine is straight. If you're sitting on a cushion, cross your legs comfortably, and if you're sitting on a chair, place your feet evenly and flat on the ground. You can rest your hands in your lap or on your thighs. Your eyes can be half-open with your gaze directed slightly downward a short distance in front of you. The most important point is to have a posture that's both upright and relaxed. The position of your body has a very direct and powerful effect on your mind. An upright posture enables your mind to rest naturally in a calm and peaceful state, and a slouched posture will make it difficult to rest your mind. Once you're sitting comfortably, the main thing is to be fully present. In other words, you have both feet (mentally speaking) inside your state of concentration—not one foot in and one foot out. Your practice is actually easier and more relaxing if you give it your full attention.

Following the Breath

There are many methods for bringing the mind to a state of concentration. I'll describe three of the most common methods, beginning with the practice of following the breath. To begin, you simply sit in a meditation posture and watch your breath. There is not much else to do. Your breathing should be natural, even, and relaxed. There's no need to alter your normal way of breathing. Then draw your attention to your breath, focusing on the coming and going of the breath at the tip of the nose and mouth. There is a sense that you're actually feeling your breath, feeling its movement.

When you do this practice, you're not just watching your breath. As you settle into the practice, you actually become the breath. You feel the breath as you exhale and become one with it. Again, you feel it as you inhale and become one with that breath. You are the breath, and the breath is you. At the end of the exhalation, let your mind and breath dissolve in the space in front of you. Allow a gap; let it go. Drop the experience altogether and simply relax in that space. Then breathe in naturally when your body is ready. There's no rush to take the next breath. Place your mind on the breath as you inhale, feel it, and relax in that space.

If your mind becomes distracted with thoughts, then mix your mind with your breath again. Focus one-pointedly, especially on the out-breath. What does one-pointed concentration mean? Imagine you're walking with a small bowl of hot oil on your head, and someone tells you, "If you spill one drop of that oil, I'm going to cut off your head!" You will certainly be focused on not spilling the oil. You will be 100 percent in the present moment. That's one-pointed concentration. In any case, the cycle simply repeats: out-breath, dissolve, gap, and in-breath. As you continue in this way, you start to feel the natural unity of breath and mind.

As you begin to relax, you can appreciate your breath. To appreciate your breath means to appreciate *nowness*, the present moment. Breathing happens only in the present. Breathe out. One moment is gone. Breathe in again. Another moment is here. Appreciating the breath also includes appreciating the world, your existence, your whole environment, and being content about your existence. It includes all of this, but basically speaking, it means appreciating the present. You're present when you're appreciating it. There's no doubt about that. So when you breathe out, simply focus; concentrate on your breath. When you breathe in, just relax and feel the breath, appreciate the present. That is meditation with the breath in a general sense. Even though you're just breathing in and out, it's an extremely powerful practice.

Counting the Breath

Whenever your mind becomes fuzzy or forgetful and the sense of nowness is gone, you can bring more precision to your awareness by a simple practice called "counting the breath." To do it, you simply observe your breathing and count each cycle of inhalation and exhalation as one breath. You can start by counting your cycles of breath from one to ten. If you find that your mind has wandered off into a thought at the count of three, for example, then you start over at one. Keep this up until you can count from one to ten without becoming distracted. You can also increase your count—to one hundred, if you like. Whatever you decide, there is the same sense of being fully present wherever you are in your count. Counting in this way strengthens your memory and increases the precision of your mindfulness. It naturally counteracts forgetfulness, because mindfulness means "not to forget."

Focusing on the Outside World

You can also practice calm abiding meditation by focusing on a visual object. In this case, everything is the same as in the practice of sitting meditation, except that your attention shifts from a purely internal, bodily experience and connects with an object in the outside world. You can use any object you like: a flower, a pebble, or your remote control. You can also use a picture or statue of the Buddha. Whatever you choose, it's best to focus on just one spot at a time; otherwise, your focus won't be clear. That spot now becomes your primary focus of attention, and your breath becomes secondary.

At first, it may seem that there isn't much purpose to looking at such objects in meditation, especially looking at "meaningless objects" like a ballpoint pen or a rock. However, this training is very important and practical, because when we come out of a meditation session, we're in the world of the senses all the time, in the midst of an ever-changing field of perception. Because this method works directly with the senses, it helps us to bring our meditative experience into the world. Once we can work with visual objects, we can rest the mind on sounds, smells, tastes, or physical sensations. However, these are trickier to work with at first because they're less substantial, so in the beginning we work with visual objects.

This type of meditation can be practiced with any object at any time. You can practice it on your way to work on the bus or subway. While the other commuters are staring at the garbage on the floor or looking at the graffiti on the walls with the goal of avoiding eye contact with strangers, you can do the same thing with the goal of increasing your awareness and peace of mind. The point is that you can bring a sense of clarity and relaxation into your experience, no matter where you are or what you're doing.

When you extend your awareness into the world in this way, it affects not only your experience of an object but also your interactions with that object. Normally when you see something, you become conscious of its color and shape; you respond with like and dislike; and you associate it through memory with other objects, people, and times. Meditating on external objects brings a clearer perception of these thoughts and emotions. It trains you to be present to your internal world and your external world at the same time. This means being in the presence of a greater range of experiences in the present moment. When you're breathing, it's happening in nowness. When you see an object, you're seeing it in nowness. Thoughts and emotions, too, exist only in this present moment. Yesterday's breath is not here. Tomorrow's breath is not here. This morning's thought is not here. Tonight's thought is not here. The picture you're looking at in any given moment is the picture of the present, of right now.

Practicing meditation in this way begins to bring about a synchronization of mind and body. Your experience of your mental and physical worlds becomes more balanced. This synchronization brings about a sense of wholeness: there's no barrier between mind and world, between your awareness and what you're aware of. This brings a sense of peacefulness, steadiness, and wakefulness to mind's agitated and cloudy states. You can get to this point using any of these methods. You can use your breath, a ballpoint pen, Buddha's image, your girlfriend's picture, your boyfriend's picture, your dog's picture, your cat's picture. It doesn't matter, as long as your mind can rest on it.

Thoughts

During your practice, the chatterbox of mind will undoubtedly open up, and you'll have lots of thoughts. Some will seem more important than others and turn into emotions. Some will be related to physical sensations—the pain in your knee or back or neck. And some will strike you as extremely important, things that can't wait. You've forgotten to respond to a critical e-mail, you need to return a call, or you forgot your mother's birthday. These kinds of thoughts will come, but instead of jumping up from your cushion, all you have to do when you're practicing meditation is to recognize them. When they tempt you with distraction, you can just say, "I'm having a thought about forgetting Mom's birthday." You simply acknowledge your thought and let it go. When we're sitting, we treat all thoughts equally. We don't give more weight to some thoughts than to others, because when we do, we loosen our concentration just enough for our mind to slip away.

I once bought a shirt at the airport because I had been traveling a long time and was in need of a change. I found one shirt in a nice, deep blue color and put it on without looking at it closely. Then, when I was sitting on the airplane, I saw it had a fish on it, along with a caption down the sleeve: "Catch and Release." I felt very good about that; it was like a message from the universe. Somehow, I was wearing instructions for working with the mind in meditation. That was my teaching for that trip, and you can use that phrase in your practice: catch your thoughts and release them. You don't need to bang them on the head and try to kill them before throwing them back. Simply acknowledge each thought and let it go.

Thoughts deserve a special mention, because we tend to forget that the practice of meditation *is* the experience of thoughts. We might think that meditation should be entirely free of thoughts and totally at peace, but that's a misunderstanding. That's more like the final result of the path than the path itself, which is the process of relating to whatever comes up for us. That's the "practice" part of the practice of meditation.

When a thought appears, we see it, acknowledge its presence, let it go, and relax. We do that over and over again. So resting the mind on the breath or an object always alternates with being distracted from it. Mindfulness brings us back to the present and to a sense of attention, or concentration. We can strengthen the power of our concentration with repeated practice, just as we strengthen the muscles in our body by flexing them when we exercise. What gives our mind the ability to flex our attention and make it strong is the breath. That's why the breath is so important in meditation.

Remember, we're working with mind, and our mind is connected to many different conditions that impact us in various, unpredictable ways. So we shouldn't expect our meditation to be the same all the time or for our progress to follow a certain course or time line. So don't be discouraged by the ups and downs in your practice. Instead of seeing them as signs that your practice is hopeless, they can help you see the need for practice and why it's so helpful.

It takes time to develop a strong state of concentration. Eventually, however, you'll see that your mind stays where you put it. Meditating and developing strength of mind isn't just a nice, spiritual activity. It's actually a great help and support to anything you want to learn or accomplish. As your mind grows calmer by practicing meditation, you experience more of what's happening in each moment. You begin to see that your life—your actual life—is far more interesting than just your thoughts about it.

ANALYTICAL MEDITATION

After developing some stability of mind in sitting meditation, you can begin to add sessions of analytical meditation to your practice. Analytical meditation is a contemplative practice. You intentionally think about something that's meaningful to you, and at the same time, you examine the way you normally think about it. Specifically, you look at a particular belief you hold and examine the logic that supports it to see if your reasoning is sound. When you do this, you're using thought as a tool to investigate your beliefs, and the more you work with this tool, the sharper it gets. In this way, your normally imprecise, confused mind eventually develops an extraordinary degree of clarity and dexterity. Many people enjoy this kind of practice, because in a way, it's like playing a game. You're outwitting the strategy of ego, which counts on your continued belief in its existence to keep you clinging to it. Analytical meditation is a practice that's associated with the third training in higher knowledge because of its power to provoke profound insights. Such insights take you beyond analysis or conceptual understanding alone to a direct perception of the mind's true nature.

In some sense, analytical meditation is like a conversation you have with yourself. You begin the conversation by choosing a topic that interests you and then asking yourself a question about it. It's important to start with a real question, one that matters to you. Whether the Beatles or the Rolling Stones are the greatest band of all time doesn't qualify. Resolving that question might be interesting, but it won't necessarily help you to put an end to your suffering in any way. However, a question like "Is there a truly existing self?" does qualify, and the answer you discover for yourself can make all the difference in your life.

Ultimately, we try to find out from this conversation what we're holding on to as a self. At the same time, we examine our own concepts and reasoning. For example, why do we assume that the "self" exists? If it exists, then where is it, and what is it made of? We take for granted that we're rational, logical beings; however, in analytical meditation, we discover gaping holes and flaws in our logic that many of our assumptions will fall through.

The most important guideline is to be honest with yourself. What do you really think, what do you really feel, what do you really see? If you can remain simple and truthful, you'll make some unexpected discoveries. As on the popular television show "CSI," you just go where the evidence leads. The following meditation instructions are examples of common assumptions and ways to analyze them.

Instructions for Practice

To begin a session of analytical meditation, take your seat and relax your mind, just as in sitting meditation. Then very mindfully bring up a thought or question to analyze. Try to stay focused on the question at hand. If your mind starts to wander from thought to thought without leading you anywhere, stop and go back to following your breath for a short time. When your mind calms down, resume your analysis as before—you don't need to start all over. At the end of the session, it's good to sit quietly again, without analysis, for several minutes. If you practice with the same question over time, it begins to permeate your being. It keeps working in the back of your mind. The answer may come when you're brushing your teeth or in the shower or in a fit of rage over your phone bill.

The Conversation: This Is Me

You might begin your analysis by bringing something to mind that the Buddha said; for example, "Although everyone believes that they have a truly existing self, that self is imaginary." Then you might think, "Although the Buddha is a reliable source and I respect his wisdom, I still feel like I have a self. It makes no sense to say there isn't a self; it's contrary to my experience. Here I am. This is me. I'm the same person I was yesterday, the day before, last year, twenty years ago, thirty years ago. In the future, I will retire and travel around the world."

If you examine this statement, then you might ask yourself, "If I'm the same self as a child, as an adult, and as a retiree in old age, then what is it that remains the same? Is my body the same? Is my mind the same? If I say that although my body is not the same, my mind is the same mind, then did my child self know everything that I know now? Is the memory of my child self the same as my memory now?"

You proceed in this way. In the idea "I am the same person," there are two related assumptions you can explore: sameness and permanence. Is permanence a requirement for a self? When you look around at the planet and the whole universe we live in, do you see anything at all that's permanent? Logically, to say that something is permanent means that it has always existed, will never cease to exist, and never changes in any respect. If it changes, then it's no longer the same, and therefore it's not permanent.

Then you might think, "Still, when I say, "This is me," I know what

I'm referring to. There is clearly a self that is one thing, which refers to me, and not to something other or someone else." But ask yourself, if that's true, then what is that one thing? Is it your body, your mind, or something else? If you say it's just your body, then you're in trouble, because then the self would have no mind—the physical organ that's the brain would be devoid of consciousness. If you say it's just your mind, then the self isn't related to the body. But clearly it's not something completely apart from these two. So you might think that the self must be body and mind together. If you say that, however, then you have to decide whether or not body and mind count as one thing. If they are one thing, then they must be the same; otherwise, they are two things. So ask yourself in what ways are body and mind actually the same? When you investigate, perhaps you see only differences. One is material and one immaterial. A body doesn't think, and a mind doesn't eat or walk around in the world. Since the self can't be just body or mind alone, it has to be both. And since body and mind aren't the same, they can't be called one thing. Therefore, the self has to be more than one thing.

You can develop a line of thought like this, and then look at it to see if it holds up. Challenge your own thinking. At this point, you could go further in looking for the self, because both body and mind themselves have many component parts; neither of them is a single, unitary thing. Could you have as many selves as there are parts of your body and mind? What would happen if you lost one of those parts—or two of those parts? If you lost an arm and your eyesight, for example, would this "I" that appears to be your self become any less of a reference point?

Next, you might think, "Okay. Maybe those aren't good reasons. But I still feel that I have a self. I have my own existence and integrity of being. I'm not a product of anyone else's thoughts or actions. Again, ask yourself, what is it within this self that's truly independent of anything else?" To what degree has your identity been influenced by your education, your family, your community, your health, or even your diet? Would you be the same or different if you had grown up in a different culture? What part of this self, including your thought processes and values, is not a product of causes and conditions? The idea of independence implies that you're self-made; it means you came as you are, and that this self of yours is not in any way a product of your environment. Is that what you really think?

In this way, we start a process of questioning and follow it as far as we can. The point is to see what assumptions we hold and what they imply. The more we find out, the less logical we seem to be. These examples are meant to point out common misconceptions we have about the self that don't hold up to reason. While they may not entirely convince us that the self doesn't exist, they at least show us how vague our sense of self is. We don't even know where it is, much less what it is. For example, when you have a headache, you say, "I have a headache." You don't say, "The body has a headache." Or if you cut your finger in the kitchen, you say, "I cut myself." In such cases, you're thinking of your body as yourself. However, when you're suffering mentally, you say, "I'm unhappy. I'm depressed. "In this case, you're regarding yourself as your mind. So sometimes we fixate on body and cling to that, and other times we fixate on mind and cling to that. In everyday life, we alternate like this all the time. Because we don't see this clearly, we become confused about who we are.

Whether you're practicing meditation to calm the mind or to examine your concepts, each session is a wonderful opportunity to get to know your mind. You don't need to approach it as something you "have" to do—that takes all the fun out of it. Meditation is actually very interesting. We hardly ever look at our mind, so when we do, it's filled with discoveries that make us curious to find out more and to get to the bottom of this thing we call "my mind."

These days people often feel they have very little time to practice meditation, but even just a little bit of practice every day has a powerful positive effect. Sitting for thirty minutes in a quiet space is very helpful, but you can do it whenever and wherever you can. You can meditate while riding the subway to work, while on hold with your phone company, or while waiting for your water to boil. Be practical about it, and just do what works for you.

appendix 2
SELECTED POEMS

Who Are You?

You are so creative
And your tricks are so original
Look at your magic
So deceptive, real, and endless.

You are a great storyteller
So dramatic, colorful, and emotional
I love your stories
But do you realize that you're telling them over and over and over?

You are such a dreamer
And you're tirelessly so passionate
For your dream characters and the world
But do you see that you're just dreaming?

You are so familiar
Yet no one knows who you really are
Are you not called "thoughts" by some?
Are you really there—or simply my delusion?

Are you not taught to be the true wisdom mind?
What a beautiful world this could be
If only I could see through this mind.

Well, it doesn't really matter
Because I don't exist without you!
"Who am I?" is perhaps the right question
After all, I'm just one of your many manifestations!

Denny's
02-07-06

True Magic

Thought . . .
You're the best actor
Hollywood has ever seen

Your dramas . . .
Have higher ratings than any soap operas on TV
Can't imagine missing any of your episodes

Your special effects . . .
Exceed the best of DreamWorks
So real they can even fool their creator

How can this world exist without your creativity?
The world would simply be empty in your absence

No Picasso, no Broadway shows
And no friends and foes

Your magic makes this world real, exciting, and alive!

Straits Café
11-11-08

BAMBOO GARDEN

Heart attempts to speak
But in the absence of words
Mind rationalizes the feeling
And finds only labels
Joy, sorrow, and depression
Heavy but paper-thin reality
So I sit like a rock
In a bamboo garden
See the sky and feel the earth
Breathe the air right here
Then I see
Clear and bright within
Love so tranquil

Café Redstar
11-13-08

notes

CHAPTER 2

1. From the *Kalamasutra*, part of the Nikaya Sutras of the Pali Canon, attributed to the Buddha. Kevin O'Neill, trans., *The American Buddhist Directory*, 2nd ed. (New York: American Buddhist Movement, 1985), 7.

CHAPTER 10

1. Maitreya, *Mahayanasutralamkara* (Ornament of Mahayana Sutras; Tib. *theg pa chen po mdo sde rgyan*), verse iv.7, with commentary by Vasubandhu. Unpublished.

CHAPTER 12

1. Hazelden Foundation. *The Twelve Steps of Alcoholics Anonymous: As Interpreted by the Hazelden Foundation*. (Center City, MN: Hazelden Foundation, 1993), 115.

CHAPTER 14

1. Patrul Rinpoche, *The Words of My Perfect Teacher* (Boston: Shambhala Publications, 1998), 129–30.
2. Ibid., 127.
3. A noted example is the work done by the Indian master, scholar, and translator Atisha, who was an important figure in the development of Buddhism in both India and Tibet. He was known as a reformer who clarified confusion and restored correctness and integrity to the tradition when he saw signs of weakness or degeneration.
4. Quoted in Unrai Wogihara, ed., *Yashomitra, Abhidharmakoshavyakhya* (Tokyo: Publishing Association of Abhidharmakoshavyakhya, 1932–36), 704.

CHAPTER 15

1. Kshitigarbha, *Dashachakrakshitigarbhasutra* (The Ten Wheels Sutra; Tib. *sa'l snying po'l 'khor lo bcu pa zhes bya ba theg pa chen po'l mdo*). See also "The Social and Political Strata in Buddhist Thought," in *The Social Philosophy of Buddhism*, Samdhong Rinpoche and C. Mani, eds. (Varanasi, India: The Central Institute of Higher Tibetan Studies, 1972), 25–35.

index